LEADERSHIP LESSONS AND REMEMBRANCES FROM VIETNAM

by

Lieutenant General Herman Nickerson, Jr., USMC (Retired)

Occasional Paper

HISTORY AND MUSEUMS DIVISION
HEADQUARTERS, U.S. MARINE CORPS
WASHINGTON, D.C.

1988

PCN 19000413000

Other Publications in the Occasional Papers Series

Vietnam Histories Workshop: Plenary Session. Jack Shulimson, editor. 9 May 1983. 31 pp. A transcript of the plenary session of a day-long series of workshops chaired and attended by government historians and archivists at the Navy and Marine Corps Historical Centers in the Washington Navy Yard.

Vietnam Revisited: Conversation with William D. Broyles, Jr. Colonel John G. Miller, USMC, editor. 11 December 1984. 48 pp. Former editor of *Newsweek* magazine and a Marine Corps veteran, Mr. Broyles discusses his return visit to Vietnam in fall 1984 with a panel of Marine Corps historians and special guests.

Bibliography on Khe Sanh USMC Participation. Commander Ray W. Strubbe, CHC, USNR (Ret.), compiler. April 1985. 54 pp. A detailed bibliography of archival sources relating to the Khe Sanh battle in 1968 including maps, documents, oral history tapes, and individual award recommendations, as well as relevant books, articles, and newspaper items.

Alligators, Buffaloes, and Bushmasters: The History of the Development of the LVT Through World War II. Major Alfred Dunlop Bailey, USMC (Ret.). 1986. 272 pp. Reproduction of a master-of-arts thesis in history at the University of Utah, presented in March 1976, by a former LVT company commander in Vietnam.

Foreword

The History and Museums Division has undertaken the publication for limited distribution of various studies, theses, compilations, bibliographies, and monographs, as well as proceedings at selected workshops, seminars, symposia, and similar colloquia, which it considers to be of significant value for audiences interested in Marine Corps history. These "Occasional Papers," which are chosen for their intrinsic worth, must reflect structured research, present a contribution to historical knowledge not readily available in published sources, and reflect original content on the part of the author, compiler, or editor. It is the intent of the division that these occasional papers be distributed to selected institutions, such as service schools, official Department of Defense historical agencies, and directly concerned Marine Corps organizations, so the information contained therein will be available for study and exploitation.

In view of his unique experiences as a senior Marine commander in Vietnam and his extensive efforts to communicate his views and his combat knowledge to the troops he commanded, it was decided to republish a series of articles that Lieutenant General Herman Nickerson, Jr., wrote in 1969-1970 while he was Commanding General, III Marine Amphibious Force (III MAF), which were published in *Sea Tiger*, the weekly newspaper distributed throughout the III MAF area of northern South Vietnam. General Nickerson commanded the 1st Marine Division in Vietnam from 1 October 1966 to 31 May 1967 and returned to that embattled country to command the III MAF from 27 March 1969 through 9 March 1970. During this latter tour of duty, in order to make up in part for an in-person briefing and welcome he used to give incoming officers and staff noncommissioned officers of the 1st Division, he began writing a series of articles for publication in *Sea Tiger*. In these short pieces, he covered a wide range of topics, some related to combat service in Vietnam, but many more to the Vietnamese people and the role of Americans in their support.

Special thanks are due to Major General Herbert Lloyd Wilkerson, USMC (Retired), who personally transcribed the articles for publication. The opinions and facts represented in this publication are those of the author and do not necessarily represent those of the Marine Corps or the Department of the Navy. In pursuit of accuracy and objectivity, the History and Museums Division welcomes comments on this publication from interested individuals and activities.

E. H. SIMMONS
Brigadier General, U.S. Marine Corps (Retired)
Director of Marine Corps History and Museums

Table of Contents

LEADERSHIP LESSONS AND REMEMBRANCES FROM VIETNAM

by
Lieutenant General Herman Nickerson, Jr., USMC (Retired)

Occasional Paper

AS I SEE
SOUTHEAST ASIA--
LEADERSHIP LESSONS AND REMEMBRANCES FROM VIETNAM

It was my custom to meet and brief personally all the new staff noncommissioned officers and commissioned and warrant officers during the time I was Commanding General, First Marine Division, from October 1, 1966, to May 31, 1967. Later, when I returned to Vietnam as Commanding General, III Marine Amphibious Force (III MAF), March 27, 1969 to March 9, 1970, this practice was no longer practical. Consequently, articles were written for the newspaper, **SEA TIGER**, which was printed by the **PACIFIC STARS AND STRIPES** in Tokyo, Japan. This newspaper had a circulation of 38,000 copies and was the best means to communicate basic messages for the troops. The following articles from the **SEA TIGER** were a substitute for personally talking with the newly arrived men and the tired and frustrated "old hands in country." The object was to remind Americans of their obligations.

But before you read the published messages, let me briefly present the essentials of my 1966-7 talk given to the new arrivals.

"Everyone has a definition in mind of freedom. As many as are here present, there are probably that many definitions of the word "freedom." You have in your own mind what freedom means to you. General Omar Bradley said it well when he wrote, 'Freedom, no word was ever spoken that has held out greater hope, demanded greater sacrifice, needed more to be nurtured, blessed more the giver, damned more its destroyer, or came closer to being God's will on earth. May Americans ever be its protector!'

"The people of the Republic of Vietnam have asked us to assist them in their fight for freedom. That is why we are here. As the days grow into months, and you become tired, frustrated and begin to doubt the worth of this effort, reach back in

2

your memories to these three words, energy, enthusiasm, and empathy.

"Most of you are young and full of energy. Energy is power, physical, mental and spiritual. Some of you are older and know you must conserve energy. Both of you need to harness this powerful energy, couple the physical energy to mental energy and temper it with the spiritual. Do not be a person full of energy but leaving the gears of his mind in neutral. The thoughtful man is the one we rely upon.

"Enthusiasm or inspiration, passion if you will, is vital to our undertaking, but it is particularly essential to the protection of freedom. It is a necessary ingredient in our esprit de corps. Remember this word, this vital ingredient when you get so tired that you just don't care what happens. Remember to use your energy enthusiastically no matter how dark the situation appears to be. Renew your energy and sustain your enthusiasm.

"Empathy may be a new word to some of you. It means, simply, looking at ourselves as others see us. It is being aware of the aspirations and needs of those we are in contact with, those we serve, and those with whom we serve. Put yourself in place of the other person and try to think as he does. This is one good way of staying alive, especially when you are able to think about how the enemy is figuring on a way of "zapping" you.

"Freedom and our sense of obligation to protect it depends on our use of our energy, enthusiasm and empathy. Never let anything that happens to you (and it probably will) steal from you your energy, enthusiasm, your empathy. And finally, just remember, any news or rumor you hear is neither as good nor as bad as the first report."

The above message to newly arrived officers and senior enlisted was worded in many ways, in the hope that it would guide their actions and aid their personal response in the difficult situations ahead.

On many occasions, I have heard it said that the war in Vietnam is the most complicated conflict in which the U.S. has been engaged. I believe this is true.

But I have heard also that there are many wars -- each separate and distinct -- being fought simultaneously in our areas of operation. In my opinion, this is not an accurate statement.

I should like you to know what I consider the true nature of the war in I Corps to be.

Our mission, as I see it, is to assist the Republic of Vietnam to govern itself as a free and independent nation.

To do this we must undertake many tasks . . . all of which must be tackled simultaneously . . . all of which must receive emphasis and attention.

As I see it, we have three main tasks confronting us in I Corps. They are as follows: first, to conduct combat operations; second, to improve and modernize the Republic of Vietnam Armed Forces (RVNAF); and third, to pacify the countryside.

Combat operations must be conducted to defeat the NVA and VC main force units thus creating a condition of security for the political and economic development of the heavily populated areas of I Corps. These operations seek out and destroy the main enemy formations, disrupt the enemy's plans and timetables, destroy his supply bases, neutralize his infiltration routes, and nullify his attempts to launch large-scale military attacks against densely populated regions. Operations such as Dewey Canyon,

5

Taylor Common, Oklahoma Hills, Maine Crag, Apache Snow--to name but a few--were launched and successfully executed to accomplish these objectives. We, and not the enemy, possess the military initiative in I Corps.

* * *

Much Accomplished - Progress Noted By III MAF CG - June 20, 1969

The announcement that 25,000 U. S. troops, including several thousand Marines from III MAF, are to be redeployed from Vietnam, I view as an encouraging sign of progress in the military situation in the Republic of Vietnam . . . progress that has been made possible through the efforts of all U. S. servicemen, past and present, who have served and sacrificed in this country for our nation's commitment to assist in bringing self-determination to the peoples of Vietnam.

As I reflect back to the situation which prevailed in I Corps just one year ago, for example, I note that enemy main force units were present in close proximity, and posed a threat to Hue, Da Nang and other densely populated areas along the coast. Today, the enemy main force units have been largely driven to the distant sanctuaries of Vietnam or to out-of-country havens in North Vietnam and Laos. Our U. S. forces, ably assisted by our ARVN comrades and other Free World forces, have met and defeated the enemy at every turn.

I note, too, that heartening and measurable progress has been made in pacification, an aspect of the struggle as vital to a successful outcome of U. S. involvement here as conventional combat operations. Through the effort s of a great many personnel, the villagers in the rural areas are now provided with greater security than they have experienced up to this time.

And finally, I note a marked increase in numbers and in the combat power and combat efficiency of our RVNAF counterparts and their paramilitary forces. The Vietnamese armed forces are now capable of assuming a larger share of the military burden . . . and we applaud them for their increased capability.

Much, therefore, has been accomplished . . . much progress has been made toward achieving our country's goals in Vietnam . . . and for this I do commend all those who have played a role in defeating the enemy in armed combat and for all other contributions made to the overall effort. The redeployment of some U.S. forces is the result.

But much remains to be done . . . much that will require the full time, talents, energies and continuing sacrifices of those who remain.

I thrust . . . I know . . . that I can count on the dedicated service of all U. S. servicemen and civilians who remain here, to see our mission through to a successful conclusion.

* * *

FROM CG III MAF - **RVN Fighting for Peace, Dignity** - **June 27, 1969**

Last week, on June 19, the Republic of Vietnam paid tribute to its uniformed men and women on its fourth Armed Forces Day. One out of every nine citizens is trained to fight the Viet Cong and the North Vietnamese Army. This boils down to six percent of the entire population. Look at it this way: if the United States had six percent of its population in uniform, it would have 12 million instead of 3.4 million in military service. Vietnam has 1,045,500.

From the southernmost reaches of I Corps right up to the DMZ, thousands upon thousands of gallant dedicated Vietnamese are waging a bitter, unwavering battle for human dignity, fighting against North Vietnamese aggression and Viet Cong terrorism, determined to achieve a lasting peace and the right of self-determination.

Those of us who have served with and fought alongside the Army of the Republic of Vietnam know of its combat efficiency, tenacity, determination to win. This is part of the reason the Army of the Republic of Vietnam elements, alone or with other Free World Forces, have successfully met the enemy in 379 battalion-sized operations in I Corps during the past 12 months . . . and, in these engagements, the Army of the Republic of Vietnam forces have accounted for 12,000 enemy KIAs, detained 2,000 enemy and captured more than 3,500 individual and crew served weapons.

The Vietnamese Navy has played an ever-increasing role in the accomplishments in the past year. Most noted perhaps was the recent combined campaign in the rivers of Hoi An. In this operation the Vietnamese Navy's Coastal Group 14, with its red-nosed, grey-hulled junks and its landing parties, joined with U. S. Navy swift boats, U. S. Marine Corps and Vietnamese Combined Action Platoons, ARVN units, Korean Marine elements and U. S. Marine Special Landing Forces in rooting out and destroying an elusive enemy.

This Vietnamese Navy will play an ever-increasing role in the combat situation in I Corps. The Vietnamese Navy operates its own Swift boats, Coast Guard cutters and support craft under its own flag.

In I Corps, the Vietnamese air power is the 41st Tactical Wing of the Vietnamese Air Force, based at the Da Nang Air Base. Many of the pilots and crew members were trained in the United States. Many have more than 2,000 combat missions over North and South Vietnam. The gallantry and bravery of the Vietnamese pilots is attested to by the numerous American decorations they have received.

Then there are the Regional Forces and the Popular Forces of the Territorial Forces of the Republic of Vietnam. These are hard-fighting units, determined to destroy the Viet Cong infrastructure in the hamlets and villages. They are the troops that, in small unit actions and in some large contacts, hack away at the VC influence and strength in their own home districts.

Other Vietnamese belong to the paramilitary groups such as the National Police, National Police Field Force, Civilian Irregular Defense Groups, Armed Propaganda Teams, the U. S. Marine Corps-initiated Kit Carson Scouts, and, while not listed as members of the Armed Forces, the People's Self-Defense Forces, numbering one million youths, women, veterans and older men.

In I Corps, it is not unusual to find families in which every member belongs to one of the above groups, doing whatever they can to defeat communism and to remove the threat to their way of life.

Throughout all of the Armed Forces of Vietnam a continuing modernization program is being accomplished. New weapons, new training, new tactics, new equipment, new and better supplies of food, clothing, tools and machinery. And with this modernization comes a major increase of Army of the Republic of Vietnam offensive operations . . . all aimed at the ultimate freedom of the Republic of Vietnam and its people.

9

We who serve in Vietnam know that a very vital part of this campaign is civic action, helping people help themselves. The Vietnamese Armed Forces take every opportunity to bring better medical and dental care to the villages and hamlets, building schools and hospitals, orphanages and churches.

These accomplishments to date are another page in the glorious history of the Republic of Vietnam's fight for freedom and self-determination. I know I speak for the entire III Marine Amphibious Force when I extend to our brothers-in-arms in the Armed Forces of the Republic of Vietnam, our sincere congratulations for past achievements, our heartiest endorsement of all their undertakings against the Viet Cong and the North Vietnamese invaders, and our sincere best wishes for continued success.

By the Republic of Vietnam Armed Forces improvement and modernization effort we increase the military effectiveness of the Republic of Vietnam fighting forces so that they can, in the future, provide for the complete defense of their country. Considerable progress has been made in equipping the Vietnamese fighting man with modern weapons. For example, all Army of the Republic of Vietnam combat units have been issued the M-16 rifle.

In I Corps, all major operations are combined; that is, they are planned and executed by Republic of Vietnam Armed Forces and U. S. Commanders and staffs. Often other commanders and staffs are involved, such as the Republic of Korea Marine Corps Brigade and the Amphibious Ready Group/Special Landing Forces. The Republic of Vietnam Armed Forces carry their full share of the load and I am pleased with their performance.

Pacification requires the close cooperation of all Vietnamese and U. S. forces and agencies. The task of pacification includes such functions as:

-The elimination of the Viet Cong infrastructure and the local guerrillas . . . those enemy who, largely through fear and terror tactics, coerce the Vietnamese villagers into supporting them.

-The establishment of local security forces to provide a close-in shield behind which the Vietnamese people can live, and work for a better existence.

-The development of the Vietnamese economy and civil government.

There are a large number of Americans in I Corps, civilians and military, as well as those of the other Free World Nations, who, in coordination with their Vietnamese counterparts, perform their tasks in a splendid manner. But there must be a uniting of all these efforts to produce the most effective results.

We, as I said, are fighting one war. There are many facets of that war. But it is still one war . . . one which requires our coordinated, combined efforts to ensure that the Republic of Vietnam is a free and independent nation.

* * *

FROM CG III MAF - Spirit of Patriots Seen in Servicemen - July 4, 1969

One hundred and ninety-three years ago today the founding fathers of our country signed a remarkable document the Declaration of Independence, in which is proclaimed that henceforth the peoples of the English Colonies in America would no longer pay allegiance to England but would chart their own course and forge their

11

own destiny.

In those critical years our ancestors actively sought and gratefully accepted help from those friends overseas who were willing to share a part of the burden to make the hopes and dreams of the peoples of this new, small, struggling nation a reality.

But those were hard years, for the struggle was bitter and intense; and not all of the colonists believed that the course was right or that the cause was worth the effort. However, in the end after much sacrifice and with the invaluable assistance provided by citizens of other lands, our ancestors successfully emerged from the struggle for independence and commenced to govern themselves as a free nation.

Almost 200 years later, this small country of Vietnam, in order to save itself from being overrun by an invading aggressor, sought help from the United States. Our government, deciding that it was in our national interests to do so, pledged help and assistance to the Vietnamese people to bring about conditions under which they could set their future course free from oppression.

In retrospect, those early American patriots were brave men; they were men of spirit, men of vision--vision to see the right cause--and determined men who were willing to fight to insure that justice prevailed. These traits have become part of our national heritage and have been passed on from generation to succeeding generations of Americans.

Yes, that American spirit is still alive and flourishing today. It is alive in the hearts of our anxious loved ones at home and it flourishes in the hearts of our fellow citizens who support and appreciate the sacrifices of our servicemen in Vietnam.

But it is here--with you men serving your Country's flag and interests in a land far from home--that the true spirit of America is most pronounced. I see it--and feel it--in my visits to the hospitals and units in the field. The troopers express their concern for their buddies and their units; and to them their own needs are insignificant.

I see this spirit of determination reflected in the fact that many thousands of U.S. servicemen have voluntarily extended their tours in Vietnam in order to become more deeply committed to the cause of freedom.

Our Country has gained much through the efforts of all U>S> servicemen who have served here. These men have proved themselves worthy successors to those early Americans who won for us the cherished possessions of freedom and self-determination--and worth successors to more recent generations of servicemen who fought to preserve our heritage for us and for all other peoples who were allied with us in the great causes of our history.

May your continued efforts be blessed with an honorable peace.

* * *

FROM CG III MAF - Team Versatility Wing's Trademark - July 11, 1969

I am impressed with the versatility and the scope of the tactical air missions that are being performed in I Corps by the members of our 1st Marine Aircraft Wing in support of our ground operations, and in this issue of the Sea Tiger, which commemorates the 28th Anniversary of the Wing's activation, I want to tell you something about these far reaching and wide ranging activities.

The 1st Wing has the equipment and the trained personnel required to perform all tasks of a well rounded tactical air arm; and all these tasks are being done, and done well, by our flying Marines. The enormous capability which is built into the Wing includes all the following facets of tactical aviation:

Tactical air command, communications and control facilities which stretch throughout I Corps.

They include forward air controllers, air liaison sections, Direct Air Support Centers, the Tactical Air Direction Center, Air Control Squadrons and Marine Air Traffic Control units which enable us to control and coordinate aviation at all levels of operations.

Offensive air. Fighter and attack aircraft--all with a wide range of ordnance--and rotary wing assault landing craft, team up to provide protection for a troop helolift in the assault, prepare the landing zones, and provide deep and close air support for our troops on the ground. Unique in our attack aircraft, we have the A-6 Intruder, which can deliver bombs with pin-point accuracy in all-weather conditions--day and night.

Rotary-wing. Helicopters give us the mobility we require in the difficult terrain of I Corps. Such jobs as logistic lifts, assault transport, close-in armed protection, emergency resupply and medical evacuation for a wounded Marine, are every day and every hour performances.

Aerial reconnaissance. Reconnaissance, observation and electronics countermeasures aircraft help us find the enemy and direct attack aircraft and other supporting arms in eliminating the threat.

Air defense. 1600 mph F-4 Phantom aircraft and Hawk missiles provide defense against enemy air attack should this materialize.

Logistics. The KC-130's inflight refueling capability allows increased time on station for our fighter and attack aircraft, and greatly increases the amount of continuous close air support that can be provided to ground troops. KC-130 and C-117 aircraft provide logistical lifts and flare drops to help both the Marine in the foxhole and supporting helicopter pilots to see the enemy at night.

I am impressed, too, by the number of developments that have been brought about by our imaginative and resourceful air-ground planners since the Korean conflict. I am talking about such things as the expeditionary airfield with all its components; the radar bombing techniques and equipment which permit bombing under all weather conditions; the logistic hardware necessary to handle the vast quantities of fuel required to keep our planes in the air; and the development of the automated equipment and procedures to insure positive control of all aircraft in an area at any time.

All of these innovations have been used in I Corps by the 1st Marine Aircraft Wing and all have proved to be highly successful developments to air-ground warfare in their combat use.

Marine Aviation has come a long way since the advent of dive-bombing during the Haiti Campaign of 1919, when Marine Lt. Lawson Sanderson discovered that

15

aiming his biplane at the target increased bombing accuracy; or, when another Marine aviator, Christian Schilt, won the Medal of Honor in Nicaragua for flying the first medevac mission under fire. It would have been difficult for the Marines of those days to imagine Marine Corps aviation as it is today.

As exemplified by the 1st Marine Aircraft Wing, it is versatile, potent, and hard hitting; and an integral component of our air-ground team which rightfully claims a large share of the credit for the success we have achieved here in I Corps.

* * *

FROM CG III MAF - Helping Them Help Themselves - July 18, 1969

In the 20 June issue of the Sea Tiger, I said that we have three main tasks facing us in I Corps, which are all facets of the One War we are fighting here. These are: first, to conduct combat operations; second, to assist in the improvement and modernization of the Republic of Vietnam Armed Forces (RVNAF) ; and third, to pacify the countryside. I want to talk to you now about this third task, pacification.

Pacification is an important word, as well as an unavoidable subject in any popular discussion of Vietnam. Yet, I believe that many Americans, here as well as at home, do not understand fully the meaning of the word as it is used to describe our activities in the Republic of Vietnam.

The work of pacification takes place behind a shield of security provided by RVNAF and Free World Military Assistance Forces (FWMAF). In conduction large scale military operations in the least populated areas of I Corps, we create a buffer zone between the Vietnamese people and the main force VC and NVA units which allows

16

the agencies of government to function.

These governmental functions involve providing local security, holding elections, and training elected officials in order that the reasonable wants and needs of the people can be fulfilled.

Briefly, this is the way it works. When an area is reasonable secure, the district chief mobilizes his assets to start the process of helping the people to help themselves. Let us be clear on what a district is--namely a geographical area within a province. (Province could be compared with one of our States and District to a County.) A district comprises several villages. Villages are also geographical areas made up of several hamlets. The village officials are elected as are hamlet officials. But it is the Village Council (of elected officials) that is given the money for projects--and the authority to govern the several hamlets of the village. Popular Force (PF) platoons, wearing brown uniforms and carrying M-16 rifles, are assigned to hamlets to assure continuing security. At the same time, Revolutionary Development (RD) cadre, clothed in black pajama-type uniforms, move into these hamlets which are under PF protection.

* * *

FROM CG III MAF - Civic Action: A Helping Hand - July 23, 1969

In contrast with the harsh and sometimes damaging effects of warfare, civic action is the way in which a military force restores the civilian community.

I have been asked, "what is civic action?" One answer is that it is the use of resources to help people improve their way of life. The term "Civic Action" may be

17

relatively new, but civic actions are as old as history. Roman Legions built roads that linked settlements and brought trade and commerce throughout Western Europe. The American pioneers who moved westward across our continent, depended upon the U›S› Army, not only for security, but for guides, for food, water, shelter and medical assistance. The U. S. Marines were instrumental helping to organize and develop local governmental agencies in Haiti and Nicaragua in the early part of this century.

History usually gives primary recognition to military feats on the battlefield, but the good works of the military done for people which may have the greatest impact upon the future of a country often go unnoticed. This is true today in Vietnam.

The scope of civic action can be great or small. It can be a major construction project or a single individual act of kindness. It can touch upon every facet of human existence--the government at all levels, the social structure, the entire economic spectrum, and the cultural traditions and beliefs of the people.

As with everything else today, civic action is far more conplex than when the Romans were pacifying Gaul or the U.S. Cavalry was confronting Indians of the plains. In Vietnam, we are among a society whose culture is much older than our own. We must therefore realize that we cannot and should not attempt to remodel the Vietnamese way of life. We must work to improve their ways and means, to help them become more efficient and proficient in providing for themselves. However, any improvement must be upon the very deep roots of their own culture, To do otherwise would destroy the foundation of their society.

We are making progress in the area of civic action, but only they can measure our success. We emphasize "self-help" in civic projects. Those things which a person himself does are his; he feels responsible fore them and will extend himself fully to maintain them. This is true of hamlet and village projects which are based on the aspirations of the people.

We can help the Vietnamese most by affording them the opportunity to help themselves. The need for a civic action project must be felt by the people and they should supply the effort and material to the fullest extent of their capacity. Our helping hand should provide that additional assistance that they cannot conceive on their own.

We support the endeavors of the Government of the Republic of Vietnam to be responsive to the needs of the people. This is a new government, which has had to give primary attention to fighting the communist enemy. Although still heavily engaged in combat operations; the government is reaching out more and more to meet the needs of the people.

I believe that our efforts in civic action are a valuable contribution to the improvement of the economic and social well-being of the Vietnamese people. I believe they have a beneficial and lasting effect.

• • •

FROM CG III MAF - Terror: When All Else Fails - August 1, 1969

Rockets land in the center of a heavily populated area and twelve persons die, seven of them children. A village police chief rides his bicycle homeward along a road south of Da Nang Air Base and is assassinated by two Viet Cong on a motorcycle.

19

A hamlet which has refused to provide assistance to the VC is attacked one night, thirty homes are destroyed and the young people kidnapped.

These are not isolated incidents, but rather frequent occurrences which are characteristic of the ruthless, immoral and inhuman nature of the Viet Cong's war of insurgency. Of course, these efforts flow from and are supported by the North Vietnamese.

But enemy acts of terrorism are rarely perpetuated in a haphazard manner. They are accomplished with specific purposes in mind, and a study of these actions and their motivations reveal a great deal about VC terrorism.

The enemy is well aware of the adverse effects his terrorists activities create. Certainly he knows that he cannot win friends with rocket attacks on civilian centers or by the assassination of respected officials. He has chosen such activity because all else has failed. The enemy would prefer the Vietnamese people to favor the Viet Cong over the legitimate Government of Vietnam, favor it through personal choice and as a result of VC nonviolent measures. However, persuasion has failed, and they have reverted to force, coercion, terrorism and murder. In this sense, widespread terrorism and murder are self-acknowledgements of Viet Cong failure.

Douglas Pike, in his highly regarded book, "Viet Cong," states that the Viet Cong planners consider terror to be the weapon of the weak, the inadequate or the desperate guerrilla leader. They believe that most objectives can be achieved without the use of terror. Yet Viet Cong terrorism continues, giving testimony to the failures of the preferred methods of insurgency.

Thomas Perry Thornton, in his essay "Terror as a Weapon in Political Agitation," states that terrorism in insurgency warfare has five objectives: to build morale within the insurgency movement; to advertise the movement among the populace; to create disunity among the people; to eliminate the opposing force; and to provoke reprisals that will have adverse reactions on the populace.

If we study these objectives, it becomes clear that certain counter-actions on our part are necessary. We, the military and the paramilitary forces, must provide security for the Vietnamese so that the terrorist successes are minimized. We must expose enemy acts of terrorism as actions of a desperate movement whose other means have failed. And, finally, we must not be provoked into thoughtless reactions by acts of terror, but rather we should contrast the enemy's policy of destruction with our own policy of nation-building.

Individually and collectively, we and the Vietnamese have a stake in the finding and eliminating of the Viet Cong terrorist. In this regard, I would be remiss if I did not mention the efforts of our Vietnamese friends. I believe that their police and military forces have done a fine job in handling VC acts of terrorism. The people in I Corps have not been intimidated by these actions of the Viet Cong. As a matter of fact, just the opposite is true. We see the Vietnamese people giving more and more support to the agencies of their government in its work of rooting out these subversive elements from their midst. The citizens of the Republic of Vietnam are recognizing terrorism as a tactic of the Viet Cong and are determined not to submit to this type of pressure.

While the Viet Cong dispense death and destruction upon the civilian Vietnamese population, Free World Forces are engaged in every imaginable humanitarian deed. While the Viet Cong, daily, demonstrate their disregard for human life and the basic welfare of the people, the GVN Forces and the Free World

Military Assistance Forces are treating the sick, improving the educational system and assisting in establishing an economic, social and political environment which will permit the individual to face the future with hope and confidence.

The contrast is obvious for all to see and judge. I am confident that the Vietnamese people will withstand the viciousness of the enemy terror and will achieve the goal they seek-the right to determine, freely, their own future.

* * *

FROM CG II MAF - Teamwork: Key to Success - August 8, 1969

In Vietnam, if there is one word that characterizes the Free World effort here, it is the word "teamwork."

"Teamwork" is an old-fashioned word, perhaps overworked in the American vocabulary; but its meaning has never had wider nor more appropriate application than right here in I Corps.

You don't have to travel far in I Corps to observe the close relationship of our troops and the Vietnamese soldiers protecting a village; or the American advisor assisting the Province Chief; or the ARVN battalion operating with the U.S. battalion; or the Vietnamese and American crew of the river patrol boat. So you recognize the teamwork.

Within the American Armed Forces in I Corps, teamwork has reached a higher level than I have ever seen before. A Marine jet guided by an Air Force FAC strikes hard at the enemy facing an Army ground unit. The Marine fire support base, out in

"Indian Country," calls and gets immediate fire support from Army and Marine artillery, the Air Force "Spooky" and the Navy gunfire support ships.

That's the operational side of things-but the same cooperation takes place in the military staffs in I Corps. On the III Marine Amphibious Force Staff we have representatives from all U. S. services. This is an integrated staff effort and produces results that are a credit to all.

But this cooperative effort is not just an American military family affair. The same cooperation exists-and vitally so-between all Free World and Vietnamese forces conducting operations in I Corps. Each day, I meet and consult with Lieutenant General Hoang Xuan Lam, the Commanding General of I Corps. Our two staffs work on every project. With common goals facing our forces, every operation in I Corps involves combined planning and combined execution.

Within the Marine Corps, teamwork is our trademark and it requires the thorough coordination of the duties and employment of every man, unit and weapon. Note such terms in our Marine vocabulary--Air-Ground Team, Battalion Landing Team and Fire-team. This teamwork serves to give the most isolated Marine rifleman the support of every weapon in our inventory.

Perhaps I have stressed the obvious. I have a reason. Teamwork is not just a prescribed method of operation, it is an essential ingredient for success. And by teamwork, I refer not only to an arrangement specified by doctrine and combat orders, but to a spirit-or state of mind. Real teamwork extends to all who serve here, all who are committed to the cause of self-determination for the Vietnamese people.

I am pleased with the teamwork I see throughout I Corps. I see it on the battlefield and in our civic and economic programs. Teamwork is our Hallmark and the key to our success. I am glad to be a member of the team.

* * *

FROM CG III MAF - Only One Color in The Corps: Green - August 13, 1969

Several weeks ago, as I was considering topics for this column, I came across the July 18th issue of the Quantico Sentry, the base newspaper of the Marine Corps Development and Education Command at Quantico, Virginia. In it was a short editorial written by a former III MAF Chaplain, Commander Richard A. McGonigal, Chaplain Corps, U›S› Navy. Chaplain McGonigal's subject is so relevant to the Marine Corps today, and his words express my feelings on this subject so well that I am taking the liberty of reprinting it in its entirety:

COLOR ME GREEN
Chaplain R. A. McGonigal

One of the Corps' most distinguished generals was inspecting a battalion. He stopped in front of a young lieutenant. "How many Negroes do you have in your platoon, son?" he asked.

"Sir, I have thirty-nine Marines in my platoon," was the answer.

The lieutenant did not realize at the time how appropriate his answer was. The General would have "had him for breakfast" if the answer had been anything else. He would have "flipped" if the lieutenant had said, "I have five Negro Marines." There are no white or black Marines. Color us green, if you must color us at all.

24

Racism has no place here.   Racism is like an unwelcome weed. It keeps creeping back when we are not looking. We catch the undertones of racism on both sides in slips of the tongue. A child on the playground will give you a hint of what his parents let slip. A word at the EM Club will drop, echoing the poison of ancient bias. Years of progress can vanish in one rumble.

Be it the duty roster, the arrangement of work details, selection for schools, disciplining, organizing a liberty trip, or assigning bunks in the barracks, we have to be on guard that old prejudices don't creep back into our decisions. We can never sleep on this problem.

Most of us have very recent memories of combat actions in which there were neither black nor white Marines--only the very welcome sight of another green uniform to the right or left. We drank from each other's canteen, donated blood, received blood, without a thought of skin pigmentation.

Indeed, the military has been the vanguard in race relations. Far ahead of the church or other agencies for a better community, the military has practiced open housing, equal opportunity employment, desegregated chapels and schools for years.

The best way to insure a peaceful liberty run is the old-fashioned "buddy system", where our buddies intercede if we get off track a bit. There's a lot to be said for using the same system on base. The instant an old wound is opened it is precisely the time for a buddy to step in and say, "Like man, cool it."

To do anything less is to forget all those white and blacks who died around us and sometimes for us. Henceforth, and always, let's color each other green.

Chaplain McGonigal wrote the above article in Quantico, Virginia, and he was talking to the Marines at that beautiful base. But certainly Vietnam and his experience with Marines here were strong in his mind as he wrote. The point he makes is most appropriate here where Marines are involved in a shooting war. There is only one color in the Marine Corps--Marine Green.

* * *

A Leader Knows
The '3 Know's'

The Marine Corps, from the very first day a recruiter set up shop in a Philadelphia tavern, has prided itself on its prowess in battle. This pride has resulted from solid achievements on the battle field. The United States Army has an equally fierce pride similarly earned.

"First in importance will be the development of a high morale and the building of a sound discipline, based on wise leadership and a spirit of cooperation through all ranks." So wrote General George C. Marshall.

The young man who serves his country today is expected to sustain the reputation of his service in combat. He excels in battle for two fundamental reasons - training and leadership. I would like to discuss this leadership as I see it here in Vietnam.

All leaders don't wear stars, leaves, bars or multiple stripes. The private and PFC look to the Lance Corporal for their survival. He is their leader. If he has learned his lessons well, the unit performs its mission. Leadership starts at the smallest unit then

26

pyramids upwards. We are all leaders--and we are or should be prepared to take charge when the situation demands. This "take charge" characteristic is one of the great strengths of our ground combat units.

With this in mind, I'd like to give you three simple rules. If you follow them, you can be a good leader. I call them the "three know's."

Know your stuff

Know yourself

Know your men

I think that when the history of our operation in Vietnam is written, we will see that our successful leaders knew these three simple rules and applied this knowledge to accomplish remarkable results. Our leaders are demanding because war is demanding and death is so final. The squad leader must demand that his men spread out, dig in, practice malaria discipline, and so on and on. But these demands produce endurance in his men and his unit does well only those things the boss checks.

Let me give you one example. I am sure you can think of others equally meaningful. Serving his second tour in Vietnam is a Marine Gunnery Sergeant named Jimmie Howard. Three years ago, Howard's unit was required to perform the impossible. He will never forget the night of 15 June 1966 - - and neither will his country. On that night, Howard, then a staff sergeant, and 17 other Marines of the 1st Reconnaissance Battalion, sat atop a hill near Chu Lai and held off a Viet Cong Battalion. The enemy attacked repeatedly throughout the night in desperate attempts to wipe out the small band of Marines. By sheer determination and firepower, welded together by Howard's inspiring leadership, every enemy assault was repulsed. In the morning, when the relief force arrived, the hill was still U. S. Marine Corps property and 39 dead Viet Cong lay close around the perimeter. Howard received the Medal of Honor for his extraordinary heroism and his men received decorations for their valor.

Howard knew his stuff, knew himself, and knew his men. He demanded the most from his men, and they produced.

Weapons improve, techniques and tactics gain in complexity, Marines and Soldiers become more specialized in the continuing evolution of warfare. But WAR has never produced a machine or an expedient that lessens the need for effective combat leadership. Nor has a substitute for brave men on the battlefield been invented. This was never more true than in Vietnam today where our future leaders are being tried and found capable!

Practice the three "knows" and inspect to insure your orders are being executed. Your leadership in combat will be equal to the test.

* * *

Kit Carson Scouts; A Place of Honor - September 5, 1969

In November 1966, while I was Commanding General of the 1st Marine Division, I witnessed the launching of a totally new Marine Corps tactical innovation in the Republic of Vietnam -- Kit Carson Scouts (KCS).

Now, nearly three years later, I am proud to look back on the heroic history and country-wide expansion of the KCS, and say "Well Done."

The former enemy soldiers serving in the Kit Carson Scouts are Hoi Chanhs who volunteer to continue to fight, now against the VC, and who have proved themselves dependable. But, most of all, they are brave, dedicated men who put their lives on the line to protect the Americans with whom they serve.

Personal bravery and professional fighting ability of "KCS" serving with Free World military forces is evidenced by the examples I record here.

In June 1967, Kit Carson Scout Throung Kinh was working with Foxtrot Company, 2nd Battalion, 5th Marines in northeastern Quang Tin Province. He was on the point when he saw NVA soldiers hiding in a rice paddy about 35 yards in front of his company. Kinh immediately opened fire on the enemy, killing four of them. He then ran into the rice paddy and engaged the remaining enemy. Some two hours later, the battlefield was swept by friendly forces and Kinh was credited with 35 confirmed enemy killed. He was instrumental in saving his company from an ambush which would have caused considerable casualties to our Marines.

Kit Carson Scout Thoung Chen, a member of a tracker dog team with the Americal Division, was assisting in a search for an enemy force in southern Quang Ngai Province in June 12 1969. As the team moved along the trail, Chen spotted the reflection of the sun off a rifle barrel. He immediately pushed the other team members off the trail and laid down a volley of fire on the suspected enemy position. Chen's immediate action saved the lives of his fellow team members and resulted in one NVA soldier killed.

Kit Carson Scout Hieu Duc Nguyen served with "C" Company, 3rd Reconnaissance Battalion, 3rd Marine Division. He has been credited with serving as the point on 32 long range recon patrols and making more than 20 kills. During contact with the enemy, Nguyen always moves in the direction of the heaviest enemy fire, courageously exposing himself to draw fire away from his fellow team members, thus enabling them to elude a numerically superior enemy force. He has been cited numerous times for his bravery, professional competence and outstanding performance of duty since becoming a KCS in April of 1968.

I recall that the first monthly report for the KCS program carried about 12 scouts on the rolls. At that time, I had great hopes that the program would be formalized throughout III MAF for I was sure we needed the advantage of the knowledge and abilities of this kind of Chieu Hoi returnee.

Today, it is a personal pleasure to know that the success of KCS has far surpassed all expectations. I am told we now have nearly 2,000 Kit Carson Scouts serving with the Free World Military Assistance Forces. These scouts have performed heroically on the battlefield, and are making a major contribution towards our ultimate success. They provide a lifetime experience and knowledge of the terrain and guerrilla tactics that no American can hope to match. This unselfish and courageous giving of this knowledge has saved countless American lives and has often tipped the scales of victory when the action has been close. Not only did they confirm their skill in combat, but they have proven to be loyal and trustworthy comrades in arms. Their performance has fully justified our faith in them. In my opinion, they have earned for themselves a place of honor in the Vietnam War. I salute them.

* * *

Ask any commander what his most enjoyable command function is, and he will almost invariably beam with pride and comment, "being able to praise my men and their accomplishments."

I particularly enjoy recognizing men and units for their valor, achievements and dedication. To this end, it is most appropriate for me to convey my admiration and compliments to the officers and men of the Third Marine Division. The "Fighting Third" is twenty-seven years old this month.

Each regiment of the Third Marine Division has its own history that began long before the Marine Corps was large enough to think in terms of divisions. But, on the 16th of September, 1942, as America and the Marine Corps faced the great challenge in the Pacific, the Third Marine Division was born. The birthplace was Camp Elliott near San Diego.

The Third Marine Division's initiation to battle was in the steaming jungles of Bougainville, largest of the Solomon Islands. The date was November 1943. In two months of bitter fighting, the Third Marine Division established its reputation. Marines of today's Third Marine Division have vivid memories of such places as Mutters Ridge, Con Thien, Khe Sanh and the Rock Pile.

On Bougainville, the never forgotten landmarks were Piva Forks, Hill 600 and Helzapoppin Ridge.

The next step was taken in the Marianas of the Central Pacific where, in July 1944, the Third Marine Division stormed ashore over the Asan beaches of the Island of

Guam-the first American territory to be recaptured in World War II. Veterans of Guam remember the Chonito Cliffs, Bundschu Ridge, and Hill 460.

The name Iwo Jima is etched indelibly in our memory. Iwo Jima ranks as one of the most violent battles in world history. This small, incredibly fortified and defended volcanic island had no rear or flanks . . . "the assault" was carried out by courageous and determined amphibious fighters. The men of the Third Marine Division were part of that force. In February and March of 1945, flanked by the Fourth and Fifth Marine Divisions, the Third Marine Division gave inspiration to the epitaph that belongs to Iwo Jima . . . "Uncommon Valor Was a Common Virtue."

In December 1945, with peace restored in the Pacific, the fighting division, that was born in war, was quietly disbanded. Appropriately enough, the division's last muster took place on the Island of Guam.

For the next six years, the Third Marine Division's colors remained cased. Then, in 1951, with another war in progress in Korea, the Third Marines soon followed by the entire Third Marine Division, was reactivated at Camp Pendleton. In 1953, the division moved to Japan to add strength to our forces in the Far East. Then, in 1956, it moved to Okinawa.

On Okinawa, the Third Marine Division was the Far East "Force in Readiness." This readiness paid off in March 1965 when the Third Battalion, Ninth Marines, landed near Danang to secure the airfield.

Since that day in 1965, the Third has fought the length and breadth of I Corps. There are few Marines in the division today who were around or even remember the battles of World War II. However, the Spirit of Bougainville, Guam and Iwo Jima still burns brightly. Our nation continues to place special trust and confidence in its Third Marine Division.

To the officers and men of the "Fighting Third," upon this twenty-seventh anniversary, I offer my heartfelt admiration and respect. You do justice to the words on your emblem-**HONOR, FIDELITY, VALOR.**

* * *

FROM CG III MAF - On Marine Mobility - September 19, 1969

Many of the Marines serving in I Corps today were very young indeed when the Marine Corps conducted history's first combat helicopter lift.

Older Marines, who have been around the Corps for a spell, will recall that it was just 18 years ago this month that Marine Transport Helicopter Squadron-161, serving in Korea, helolifted 224 Marines, including a heavy machine gun platoon, and nearly nine tons of cargo during Operation SUMMIT.

Besides being a "first," the helolift of Operation SUMMIT was indicative of the Marine Corps' constant striving for increased mobility. The Marine Corps has always accented mobility from the days of "Old Ironsides" to mules in Nicaragua and so on down to the present.

In the early years of the Corps, the Marine Corps realized the potential of the amphibious landing. Our initial "mobility" from ship to shore was the muscle-powered ship's whaleboat. With the advent of the machine age, muscle-power gave way to motor power.

With World War II on the horizon, and the amphibious assault firmly recognized as a necessary tactic for victory, the Marine Corps, in conjunction with the Navy, developed the landing craft with the bow ramp-the first water craft specifically designed for the assault landing of troops. This craft, the LCVP, is still with us today.

As we refined further our amphibious techniques early in World War II, it became apparent that a vehicle was needed that would not have to pause at the water's edge, but could continue to move assault troops inland for rapid development of the beachhead. Thus, under Marine Corps impetus, the amphibious tractor"Amtrac"- was born.

But, by 1946, something new was happening. Vertical flight-the helicopter-came into being. Imaginative Marines started viewing heliborne landings as the next step. This new mobility would allow us to deliver our men and equipment further inland, around the enemy's defenses, to a location behind him.

However, it was 18 years ago this month, that the Marine Corps Air-Ground Team-and the amphibious assault- really took on a new dimension. As we view the gaggles of helicopters in I Corps today, carrying out every conceivable tactical and logistical mission with all our forces, we are seeing the offspring of Operation SUMMIT come of age. The helicopters we used in Korea were not of the size and speed of today's jet helicopters. But experiments and theory have a way of becoming facts. Vertical envelopment, a Marine Corps concept, has worked and worked well.

Mobility is the key to our air-ground team. We see it in the designs and uses of all our equipment, in the development and application of our skills, and in the planning and tactics of our operations, large or small, combat or non-combat. For the Marine Corps, this capability of conducting highly mobile operations is an essential element in successfully executing our assigned missions.

Our expertise in amphibious operations makes maximum use of mobility and flexibility. Rapid movement by water, surface and air exemplifies our operations in Vietnam. Infantry elements are quickly emplaced, then supplied and supported by the whole spectrum of machines and techniques available to the Corps. Operation DEWEY CANYON is an excellent example to study. In and out of Vietnam, we exist as a highly mobile and flexible strike force, capable of immediate response whenever and wherever the situation demands.

What is next? As long as there are imaginative and forward looking Marines, there will be newer, faster and better means of tactical movement. Readiness has made our Corps famous. The key to readiness is mobility. It's our way of life.

Next week, I will discuss the U. S. Army's employment of helicopters. This application of mobility has revolutionized the Army's battlefield . . . and is a great step forward.

* * *

FROM CG III MAF - Army Air Mobility - September 26, 1969

The helicopter has become so commonplace in our daily operations that I'll bet you don't look up when you hear its distinctively familiar clop-clop trademark. I know I did in Korea since it meant my Division CG was arriving!

Although such a situation might have been hoped for by Harold F. Pitchairn when he pioneered the autogyro and flew the first one on December 19, 1928, at

Philadelphia. I doubt that he foresaw the effect his wheezing machine would have on modern warfare.

From this meager beginning, U. S. technology has developed the superb flying machines as we know them today. Choppers themselves have spawned to military terminology such conglomerate verbiage as "Airmobile", "Air Cavalry", "Aerial Rocket Artillery", and "Aero-rifle troop". These are not Hollywood terms, but official titles designating Army units so equipped and trained as to add a new dimension to the use of the helicopter. Probably without realizing it, all of you have worked with, or observed these units operating in the III MAF zone, because they are, in addition to the usual infantry, artillery and supporting units, organic to the U. S. Army's 101st Airborne Division (Airmobile)-one of two Army airmobile divisions.

The airmobile division has more than 400 organic helicopters, light observation, flying crane, Huey, Cobra and Chinook. This division is designed to have a flexibility and versatility limited only by weather and the understanding and imagination of the commander. The key to success is the helicopter which provides the commanders with an unprecedented capability to position up to battalion-size units virtually anywhere on short notice and then to support the force operationally and sustain it logistically. Specifically, the Air Cavalry Squadron of an airmobile division, with its light observation helicopters, aero-rifle troops and ground elements, constitute the commander's primary reconnaissance element. The Aerial Rocket Artillery Battalion, with Cobra gunships armed with rockets, a minigun and a 40mm grenade launcher, provides close and responsive fire support for the infantry. The Aviation Group provides the flying crane with its eight ton lift capability and the CH-47 Chinooks which can carry 33 troops or four tons of cargo. Interwoven throughout are the familiar and hardworking Huey gunships and slicks which transport troops and supplies, serve as a communication platform for command and control, and provide fire support from two M60 machine guns.

These units, along with infantry and artillery, can be organized into task forces of various sizes, or employed as a part of a battalion or brigade (regimental) combat team. They can, within themselves, be a quick reaction force-or they can deliver an outfit formed from other organic units. It does not take much imagination to visualize the combinations in which these units can be employed so as to maximize their capabilities to take an objective.

An interesting aspect of Army aviation is that pilots are not in a separate "branch" but rotate tours between flying and ground assignments. Thus, the infantry officer who is a Cobra pilot for one tour might be assigned as an infantry company commander for the next. In fact, in an airmobile division, the commanding general and his assistant division commander are usually helicopter qualified.

I hope this thumb-nail sketch of the more basic aspects of an Army airmobile division adds to your professional education. The success of the 101st Airborne Division (Airmobile) in its numerous operations as a member of the III MAF team is clear evidence of the effectiveness of the airmobile concept.

* * *

FROM CG III MAF – Vietnam's Marines – October 3, 1969

A few days ago, on October 1, the Vietnamese Marine Corps celebrated its 23th anniversary.

Although their history is brief, it is one which Lieutenant General Le Nguyen

Khang, seventh Commandant of the Vietnamese Marine Corps, and all the men who serve in the organization can be proud of their unit's accomplishments which span 15 years of hostilities and combat.

It was shortly after the 1954 Geneva Accords that the Republic of Vietnam recognized the need for a Marine Corps, and on October 1, 1954, the NVMC was activated as a component of the Vietnamese Navy, and was assigned the mission of conducting amphibious operations on the coast, rivers and canals.

During this early phase, the Vietnamese Marine Corps consisted of 1,137 Vietnamese, and one U. S. Marine Corps advisor, who constituted the personnel strength for a landing battalion, river patrol company, river group, ranger group and field support group.

About 11 years after its birth, the Marine Corps was officially separated from the Vietnamese Navy, and on January 5, 1965, it became an autonomous service under the control of the Joint General Staff of the Vietnamese Armed Forces.

Like any youngster, the Corps grew through the years until today it is a force of nearly 9,000 officers and men who have been organized into a Division Headquarters, a Training Command, six Infantry Battalions (with four rifle companies per battalion), two Brigade Headquarters, two Artillery Battalions, a Medical Battalion, a Headquarters Battalion and a Service Battalion.

As we Marines are all aware, the higher up the ladder you advance, the more responsibility you receive. This is true with the mission of the VNMC, which has been expanded to: (1) Conduct amphibious operations throughout the coastal areas and off shore islands of the Republic of Vietnam; (2) Conduct riverborne operations along the coastal lowlands and in the Delta Region; and (3) Conduct such independent and/or joint combined ground operations in conjunction with Republic of Vietnam Army and Free World Forces as may be directed.

Patterned after our own Corps, the Vietnamese Marines have proven their capabilities by executing major troop movements on land, sea and air. They are part of the Republic of Vietnam General Reserve, and have been employed from the DMZ to the Mekong Delta-operating in all four Corps Tactical Zones.

During one engagement in northern I Corps, during 1965, the 2nd Battalion, VNMC, exhibited a fighting spirit which was recorded by the enemy, when the capture of his documents revealed the notation, "The second Battalion . . fought like Crazy Water Buffaloes." The 2nd Battalion, incidentally, is the most decorated unit in the Vietnamese Marine Corps, and their decorations include a United States Presidential Unit Citation.

If you happen to be traveling through some village or hamlet and see a poster proclaiming, "Serve with the Best," don't be alarmed that one of our recruiting sergeants has set up a shop here in Vietnam. "Serve with the Best-Be a Vietnamese Marine," is a recruiting pitch used by 15 recruiting teams traveling throughout the four Corps Tactical Zones.

The VNMC is an all-volunteer unit, and the men who join the "Corps" must virtually sweat blood in order to graduate from the intensive Vietnamese Training Center at Thu Duc, near Saigon. The center is modeled after our own Marine Corps Recruit Depot, and most of Thu Duc's Drill Instructors are graduates of our DI School in San Diego.

39

There's no greater tribute an enemy can pay to the opposite force than to give the organization a distinctive nickname. In World War I, we earned the title "Devil Dogs." Here, in Vietnam, our counterparts have earned the title Trau Dien "Crazy Water Buffaloes."

I for one, am extremely proud to see the Devil Dogs and Crazy Water Buffaloes fighting a common enemy.

* * *

FROM CG III MAF. - A Primary Goal - October 10, 1969

In my first column in the Sea Tiger, I states that Free World Forces were fighting one war in Vietnam, but this war involved struggles on many fronts-not all on the battlefield. A primary goal of the Government of the Republic of Vietnam is to organize its strength for its future as a free nation. As in all nations, the real strength of the Republic of Vietnam lies in its people. It is ten of utmost importance that attention and concern be given to the political unit that contains the vast majority of the Vietnamese people-the village.

It is also in the village that American fighting men come into close contact with the people. If we are to assist the Vietnamese in their struggle for political, civic and economic progress, it is fundamental to our effort that we understand-and respect-the village political structure.

The rural village is the lowest formal level of government in this country. It is referred to as the basic administrative unit in the Republic of Vietnam. The Republic's constitution refers to only three levels of local government-city, province and village.

In August 1969, there were about 2,500 villages throughout the Republic of Vietnam, and they are responsible for governing more than 13,000 hamlets. Thus, the majority of the Vietnamese people are served by village government.

The "mayor", or executive of a village is the village chief. This is an appointive office, and is often filled by a respected village elder. Since 1966, the village administrative functions have been performed by an administrative committee composed of a chairman (the village chief), vice chairman, and staff members. Each staff member is in charge of certain functions such as administration, agriculture, security and military affairs. The members of this committee are appointed by either the village chief or the province chief. In essence, this administrative committee is the village chief's staff.

The village chief's committee is complemented by the village council which is an elective body of six to twelve nonsalaried councilors and to which the village chief and his administrative committee are responsive. In fact, this council, which usually meets once a month, is the decision making arm of the village government; whereas the village chief and his committee are the implementing arm. The council may be dissolved by the province chief if there is evidence of more than half of the council members being pro-communist-a measure designed to keep Viet Cong influence out of the local community. A councilor may be dismissed for the same reason, without eliminating the council.

In recent weeks, the central government has turned over to most of the villages, checkbooks for the spending of millions of piasters on project, and thereby encourage popular participation in local self government. "Town meetings", long a successful method of conducting public business in New England communities, have brought together for the first time people with common interests in community development.

With responsibilities increasing daily, village officials have long needed some type of formal training. This need is being met. Hundreds of local officials in I Corps have completed or are now attending training in leadership and administration at the National Training Center at Vung Tau. Others have been or are being trained in province schools. The result has been increasingly capable village administration responsive to the people.

The struggle to bring political and economic stability and progress to the people of Vietnam is no less important than the military effort in the field. The enemy is aware that he cannot win if he loses the struggle in the villages. He has placed increasing emphasis upon the destruction of the legitimate village political structure by assassination and subversion. The enemy knows that a strong and prosperous village, loyal to the national government, can effectively thwart his design to subjugate this nation. We, as members of the Free World Military Assistance Forces, must do our utmost to assist the Government of the Republic of Vietnam in the winning of this struggle at the village level.

I am providing further details to all commands of II MAF on the organization and functioning of the Republic of Vietnam. I ask you to read and understand this material, especially what has been outlined here.

We are winning. We need only persevere.

. . .

We in the III Marine Amphibious Force have watched a transformation take place in the Republic of Vietnam Armed Forces (RVNAF).

We have seen these gallant fighting men quickly become proficient with the most sophisticated weapons in the free world's arsenal . . . weapons that took us years to perfect and master.

Only a few years ago, the average Army of the Republic of Vietnam (ARVN) maneuver battalion was armed with M1 rifles and carbines. The Republic of Vietnam Armed Forces (RVNAF) were still in the experimental stages of artillery and air support, and motor transport sections contained few vehicles.

Today, all maneuver battalions of the RVNAF have been equipped with M-16 rifles, and it is expected that by the end of this year the battalions will be fully equipped with M-60 machine guns and M-79 grenade launchers. Also their PRC-9 and PRC-10 radios are being replaced with newer, lightweight PRC-25's.

In 1968 alone, the RVNAF increased their motor transport capability fifty percent, and armoured personnel carriers and other armoured vehicles increased by thirty-five percent. This increased transportation has allowed the ground forces to shoulder greater responsibilities.

Two weeks ago I spoke about the Vietnamese Marines and the giant strides they were making. I won't repeat their accomplishments in this article.

Marines are aware that air support can often mean the difference between

43

success and failure. The Republic of Vietnam also realizes this and the Vietnamese Air Force (VNAF) has increased from an initial 32 aircraft to more than 350.

Today's VNAF has qualified pilots flying the F-5 "Freedom Fighter", A-37 attack bomber, C-119 "Flying Boxcar", UH-1 "Iroquois" helicopter, A-1H "Skyraider", C-47 "Skytrain" and light observation aircraft.

Progress is also being made in the Vietnamese Navy (VNN). They received 64 U. S. Navy river gunboats in mid-1969. This brought the total of craft turned over to VNN since June 1968 to 167.

Modernization, however, is not simply supplying arms, ammunition, supplies and equipment. These necessities would be wasted if there were no qualified personnel to maintain the gear. Comprehensive training programs, both in Vietnam and out of country, have been established-to provide qualified technicians for practically every need.

Has all this paid off? You bet it has. Let me cite but one example. From April 19 to June 13, 1969, in operation LAM SON 274, the 7th Armored Cavalry Regiment located in Northern I Corps killed 112 NVA and detained 7 while suffering seven killed and 38 wounded.

The Vietnamese officers and enlisted, in collaboration with our military advisors, have worked hard to modernize the Armed Forces of the Republic of Vietnam. Now they see their results. They see it in the determination of the individual Vietnamese Soldier, Marine, Airman, Sailor and RF/PF. All have proved that they are shouldering more and more of the load.

In fact, through modernization, the Vietnamese Armed Forces are saying, loud and clear: "We can do more, we ask you to do less."

* * *

FROM CG III MAF - U. S. Navy in I Corps - October 24, 1969

On October 17, 1969, we will celebrate Navy Day and I can think of no more appropriate time than now to recognize the presence of the U. S. Navy in I Corps.

It was only four years ago, October 15, 1965, that the Navy began turning the sand beaches around Danang into suitable off loading ramps, and developing this natural harbor into a major deep water port.

The tasks performed by the Navy are many, but their primary mission is supporting our Marines and soldiers ashore. This is being done in an outstanding manner.

The Navy ashore in I Corps numbers more than 22,000 men. The biggest organization is the Naval Support Activity (NSA) which provides logistical support throughout the five northernmost provinces of the Republic of Vietnam.

The motto of NSA is "They shall not want." From what I have seen no one wants among the 180,000 U. S. and Free World Forces in I Corps.

In addition to craft supplied for cargo transportation and harbor service, NSA supplies I Corps with fresh, dry and fresh provisions, spare parts and hundreds of other items.

The link between our fighting men and their supplies is provided by widely dispersed NSA detachments. Men of these detachments move the cargo from the ships and boats to waiting Army and Marine Corps trucks for delivery to you, the customers in the field.

In addition, medical aid is provided around the clock. The NSA Station Hospital provides Marines and Soldiers expert medical care also. Wounded men are treated on hospital ships Repose and Sanctuary, which can be reached within minutes by helicopter.

NSA has a huge Public Works Department with approximately 6,000 employees. Public Works provides maintenance, transportation and utilities support in selected areas throughout I Corps.

But the Navy's support is more than service support . . . it is combat support also. I am sure that many of you have benefited from the tremendous firepower provided by the gunfire support ships of the Seventh Fleet off the coast.

The 3-5-6-8 and 16-inch guns of Navy destroyers, cruisers and a battleship have provided additional firepower necessary to the successful accomplishment of our mission. All but New Jersey stand ready to provide fire power and to protect against submarine, air and surface threats.

If Navy close air support is needed, planes from the carriers off the coast are just minutes away.

Other Navy men are serving along the I Corps coastline in Swift Boats of

Operation Market Time. The Swifts have been extremely effective on the Cua Dai River south of Danang.

The versatile River Patrol Boats and other small boats of Commander Task Force Clearwater provide security on the Perfume River near Hue and along the Cua Viet River near the DMZ.

Operating in support of these boats are NSA's PBR Mobile Base One at Tan My and the Small Craft Repair Facility at Danang. Skilled sailors at these two locations provide boat maintenance support ranging from hull repair to engine overhaul.

Navymen are busy helping their Vietnamese counterparts, too. Extensive training programs prepare Vietnamese Sailors to repair, maintain and operate craft which will eventually be turned over to the Government of Vietnam.

Another group which is familiar to all of us and which deserves recognition for many jobs well done is the Navy Construction Brigade Seebees. I shall discuss this important group in a later column.

The role of the U. S. Navy in I Corps is one vital to all of us. I salute them for their contribution to the people of the Republic of Vietnam.

* * *

FROM CG III MAF - Psyops-Truth As A Weapon - October 31, 1969

Our operations in III MAF confront us with many new and changing situations. I am continually impressed with the way Soldiers, Sailors, Airmen and Marines of III

MAF adapt, develop new procedures and perform, their missions in these changing situations. One of the more important of our many new experiences involves the close contact we have with the people of the Republic of Vietnam in whose land we serve and whose lives we help protect.

Security for the people of the Republic of Vietnam is an essential part of the overall purpose of the US and Allied Forces. We fight here to make it possible for the people of this Republic to decide their own future.

When we consider our contact with the people and our purpose here, in comparison with the enemy and his contacts and purposes, the difference between the two viewpoints is startling. The enemy terrorizes; we protect. The enemy destroys; we build.

The enemy terrorizes by murdering noncombatants, old people, women and children, in his attempt to cause the people to submit to his will through fear.

Along with the Government of the Republic of Vietnam and our Allies we keep the enemy away from the villages and homes of the people by our combat actions, security patrols and a wide range of actions by such forces as Combined Action Platoons.

The enemy destroys homes, schools, temples and markets by burning, explosive charges and shelling. He also attempts to destroy the body and the spirit by maimings, abductions, confiscation of food and suppression of thought.

We help to build through a variety of civic action programs. Our assistance to schools and orphanages and the very effective programs of our MEDCAP and DENTCAP are examples. The Republic of Vietnam Armed Forces and III MAF Forces have defeated the enemy at every turn, while at the same time they have provided security for the people and helped them rebuild their homes and their lives. All of these efforts and successes convince us that the Government of the Republic of Vietnam offers a far better way of life for the people of Vietnam than does the oppression of the enemy. Most of the Vietnamese people know the VC as their enemy--the enemy of Freedom and justice.

Yet there are those among us who are VC or VC sympathizers. We want to help these folks realize the truth of the enemy's actions and issues. How do we get such messages across? Our main method of delivery of the message is through Psychological Operation, or PsyOp, which tells the truth about the true nature of the war to all the people, friendly, enemy and neutral. Friendly audiences are informed of combat successes by the GVN and allied armed forces. The enemy is continually informed of the fact that he is an invader, not wanted in South Vietnam, and is urged to choose the right cause and rally or "Chieu Hoi" to the GVN. Neutral audiences are informed of our success and enemy failure.

PsyOp uses leaflets, handbills, posters, newspapers, loud-speaker broadcasts, television, radio and motion pictures to deliver these messages.

But, as with our other operations, the most vital resource is the individual who engages in face-to-face contact with people. This requires a high degree of understanding and personal response.

Our actions and deeds must be consistent with our statements. Then it becomes the whole truth and becomes believable to the people who hear the messages. Our behavior helps them to perceive things, to learn from their own observation of us.

49

Our deeds provide the spark that gives life and meaning to the entire PsyOp effort.

We deal with the people in their villages with a variety of programs and contacts, such as Combined Action Program and civic action projects. But the most important resource is the individual American. When we show friendship, courtesy and understanding, we reinforce the meaning of our actions, and make clear that our aims and methods are different from those of the enemy. We protect and build to help the people realize a brighter future.

If we fail to show the proper respect to village chiefs, even though the act we are performing is a helpful one, we cause resentment in people. The enemy uses such acts in his propaganda efforts to destroy the faith the people have in us and their confidence in their own future.

I am confident that we will continue to defeat the enemy in combat. I am also confident that we will continue , with empathy, our acts of kindness and understanding. Such a combination cannot fail.

* * *

FROM CG III MAF - **Marine Corps Birthday - November 7, 1969**

On this 194th anniversary of our Corps, I think it is fitting to use my column to bring you the words of a former Commandant of the Marine Corps . . . an officer who, by every deed and every thought, exemplified a model of leadership for us all to follow. On this Marine Corps Birthday, let us re-read the words of Major General John A. Lejeune, 13th Commandant of the Marine Corps.

50

"On November 10, 1775, a Corps of Marines was created by a resolution of the Continental Congress. Since that date many thousands men have borne the name Marine. In memory of them it is fitting that we who are Marines should commemorate the birthday of our Corps by calling to mind the glories of its long and illustrious history.

"The record of our Corps is one which will bear comparison with that of the most famous military organizations in the world's history. During 90 of the 146 years of its existence the Marine Corps has been in action against the Nation's foes. From the Battle of Trenton to the Argonne, Marines have won foremost honors in war and in the long era of tranquility at home generation after generation of Marines have grown gray in war in both hemispheres, and in every corner of the seven seas that our country and its citizens might enjoy peace and security.

"This high name of distinction and soldierly repute we who are Marines today have received from those who have preceded us in the Corps. With it we also receive from them the eternal spirit which has animated our Corps from generation to generation and has been the distinguishing mark of the Marines in every age. So long as that spirit continues to flourish Marines will be found equal to every emergency in the future as they have been in the past."

These words were written in 1921 but they are just as applicable and timely today. They sum up the esprit and dedication of our Corps.

Happy Birthday, Marines.

* * *

Inscribed on the tomb of the great architect Sir Christopher Wren in St. Paul's Cathedral, London, is a simple statement:

"If you seek a monument, look about you."

And if you look about you, in London, you will see the handiwork of the greatest of all British architects. His creations are there for all to see.

When the Navy's Construction Battalions (Seabees) finally depart from I Corps, they, too, will need no monuments to their deeds. Like Sir Christopher Wren, their accomplishments can be seen by simply looking around. Airfields, camps, bunkers, bridges and roads built by the Seabees dot the landscape from the DMZ to the II Corps border.

The paving of National Highways One and Nine represents one of the most significant combat engineering feats of the Vietnam War.

Since first arriving in I Corps, the Seabee story has been one amazing episode after another. The Marines landed at Chu Lai on May 7, 1965. Following them ashore over pontoon causeways laid down by Amphibious Construction Battalion One were the men and equipment of Mobile Construction Battalion Ten (MCB-10). In around the clock activity, the Seabees cleared and graded the strand for a 3,500 foot aluminum-plank tactical airfield which was rapidly installed. The installation of the aluminum matted field made possible an early and unremitting pressure on enemy targets. This enabled the Seabees to build further facilities which immeasurably aided the Marines in securing the Chu Lai area. That, of course, was only the beginning. Since that time their countless accomplishments have included the construction of berthing and messing facilities for 125,000 men, 138 miles of road, 237 wells, 73 bridges and millions of square feet of storage space. The list goes on and on.

Since the initial landing of Navy Mobile Construction Battalion Ten in the spring of 1965, the Seabee force has numbered as many as 12 battalions. They operate under the control of Commander, Third Naval Construction Brigade here in Danang.

Camp sites are located throughout I Corps.

The Seabees have also used their skills to assist the people of the Republic of Vietnam. They have helped to construct numerous schools and hospitals. At the same time, tens of thousands of pounds of food, clothing, soap, school supplies, and other needed items have been distributed to the villages, schools and orphanages near Seabee camps.

Special Seabee teams composed of a Navy Civil Engineer Corps Officer, 11 constructionmen, and a Navy Corpsman, have instructed and assisted local villagers to construct buildings, bridges, roads, dams, wells and sewerage systems. When the Seabees leave, these construction skills will remain.

Let's take a look at the individual. What makes a Seabee? In their own words: "A Seabee is a soldier in a sailor's uniform, with Marine training, doing civilian work at WPA wages." But for my money, Seabees are a lot more than their own definition implies. The spirit that was at Guadalcanal and Iwo Jima and Inchon lives on with the Seabees in Vietnam.

We in the military have always fought and worked together as a team. Speaking for all of us I am grateful for the 'Can Do' attitude of our team mates, the Seabees, who built, among other things, the airfield at Chu Lai, contonments throughout I Corps and our bases at Dong Ha and Quang Tri.

One World War II commander said of the Seabees: "The difficult they do at once; the impossible takes a little longer." I might add, not much longer.

• • •

FROM CG III MAF – Supporting Arms-The Winning Ticket – November 21, 1969

Napoleon in his Maxims of War said:

"The better the infantry, the more it should be economized and supported by good batteries."

While this statement was made in 1831, no battlefield commander in the Free World Forces would argue with it today. All of our commanders know that supporting arms are the winning ticket just as they were in the days of Napoleon. We in the Free World Forces consider the expenditure of bombs and shells mandatory in order to minimize our casualties.

The war has, more than any other, provided the formula for testing the true worth of a commander. Can he effectively employ his supporting arms? Can he make the enemy pay dearly while conserving the lives of his fighting men?

Here in I Corps, fighting the North Vietnamese Army, we confront a dedicated foot soldier, but a soldier lacking in supporting arms. He has mortars,rockets, small arms, automatic weapons, grenades, mines and booby traps but only limited artillery support and no air or naval gun fire. The test of a North Vietnamese commander,

54

then is to counter our overwhelming firepower. He doesn't mind losing troops to gain his limited objectives.

The test of the Free World Troop Commander is not so simple. He must effectively employ weapons that span the spectrum from 60mm mortars and 8 inch naval guns to 2,000 pound bombs. In each confrontation with the enemy, he must determine rapidly what supporting arms are available, which are the best weapons to employ, and then coordinate their use with all agencies involved. We have the resources. We must use them properly. Those of us who do not use our artillery, air, naval gunfire in seizing objectives are not professionals. No leader, from squad leader to division commander, can say he is truly a "pro" unless he consistently brings the maximum fires down upon the enemy. This is proper protective reaction.

I've talked enough. Let the facts speak for themselves. Here are three examples of the effective use of supporting arms as reported in the U.S. press:

"A reconnaissance element of the First Marine Division spotted 26 enemy soldiers moving in the open southeast of An Hoa. The Marines called in artillery fire that killed five NVA soldiers. There were no U.S. casualties."

"A reconnaissance element of the 196th Infantry Brigade observed seven enemy soldiers moving east of Tam Ky. The soldiers directed mortar fire on the enemy, killing five. There were no friendly casualties."

"An element of the 3d Marines was hit by small arms fire and 60mm mortars southwest of Dong Ha by an estimated force of 30 North Vietnamese soldiers. The Marines called in air strikes. Ten North Vietnamese were killed while one Marine was wounded."

* * *

55

Inscribed on the National Archives Building in Washington, D. C., are the words: "What's past is prologue." Whatever achievements have taken place in the past should lead to greater accomplishments in the future.

If the statement "What's past is prologue" has any validity, then the future of the Navy's Chaplain Corps is indeed bright. Ships, men and women have changed over the years but the Navy chaplain has provided and continues to provide comfort and spiritual guidance to our servicemen in the time honored tradition of the Corps.

There are over 1,000 Navy chaplains serving Navy, Marine Corps, Coast Guard and Merchant Marine personnel and their families afloat and ashore, all over the world. Their story is much too long to cover in a few sentences so I will limit my remarks to their affiliation with the U. S. Marine Corps, the story I know best.

It's perhaps symbolic that the Navy Chaplain Corps should have been organized 194 years ago on November 28-only a few days after the founding of the Marine Corps.

Official records indicate that the first chaplain assigned full time to the Marines was a Protestant chaplain named Bower R. Patrick, who was ordered to the Atlantic Fleet's Marine Expeditionary Force in April 1914.

During the years that followed, chaplains accompanied Marines from the battlefields of Europe to the ancient cities of China. In World War II, 16 chaplains were assigned to each of the six Marine divisions. By the time of the Korean conflict, 26 chaplains were serving with each of our divisions. Wherever Marines go in defense of freedom, Navy chaplains also go ministering to their spiritual needs, sharing their dangers and accomplishments.

In addition to his normal ministry, the Navy chaplain in I Corps is deeply involved with the people of the Republic of Vietnam. Through the III Marine Amphibious Force Chaplain Civic Action Program, he identifies specific areas of need within the civilian community. Because of his efforts, scores of schools, hospitals, orphanages, churches, and similar institutions have been constructed and thousands of tons of supplies and materials have been distributed to needy Vietnamese.

Thus, today as through the years, the Navy Chaplain Corps continues to follow a tradition of service and sacrifice, sharing the same deprivations and hazards as the Marines and, when called upon, making the supreme sacrifice. Let me cite but one example.

On September 4, 1967, Lt. Vincent Capodanno, CHC, USNR, was serving with the 3d Battalion, 5th Marines in Quang Tin Province. In response to reports that the 2d Platoon of "M" Company was in danger of being overrun by a strong enemy force, the chaplain left his position of relatively safety and ran across an area raked with fire to join the platoon. Despite enemy small arms and mortar fire, he moved among the platoon giving aid to the wounded and comforting the dying.

Painfully wounded himself by a mortar round he continued to calmly move about the battlefield providing encouragement to the platoon. seeing a wounded corpsman directly in the line of fire, he moved to assist him when he was mortally wounded by machine gun fire inches from the corpsman. He gallantly gave his life in the service of God and Country.

On January 7, 1969, Chaplain Capodanno was awarded the Medal of Honor posthumously for his actions with the 5th Marines.

I congratulate all Navy chaplains serving throughout the world on this, their 194th anniversary. By their selfless dedication throughout the years they have indeed made the past a prologue to the future.

* * *

FROM CG III MAF - How I View The CAP - December 3, 1969

Americans have always been great innovators on the field of battle. I predict that future historians will agree that one of the most successful innovations of the war in Vietnam was the Combined Action Program.

Today the NVA and VC units in I Corps operate in relatively unpopulated areas and avoid large scale battles. Our conventional tactics have forced them into this position. Their losses have been great. Yet those who are farmers by day and Viet Cong by night are relatively immune to conventional warfare tactics. As fish in a pond become scarce when threatened by a horde of fishermen, large scale search and clear operations usually net few of the elusive local VC. These guerrillas must be painstakingly targeted by friendly forces living in the villages and hamlets.

The Combined Action Platoons (CAPs), by operating in small groups, patiently and using their ingenuity, find the "fishing" profitable in their villages. As proof of this, in the first nine months of 1969, the 144 CAPs deployed in I Corps killed more than 1700 of the enemy and captured more than 300 prisoners and 790 weapons.

The first CAP was formed near Phu Bai in 1965, thus inaugurating the unique union of Vietnamese Popular Force and U. S. Marines. A platoon of Popular Force Soldiers (PFs) constitute the Vietnamese portion of the combined platoons. The Marine element is a rifle squad with a Navy Corpsman attached. The PFs are local soldiers and receive little pay and formal training. However, they possess an incomparable military asset: the will to win. Assigned to their home villages and hamlets, the PFs have a personal stake in eradicating VC terror. After a full day in their shops or on their farms, the PFs sacrifice their nights to patrol and ambush with members of the Marine Rifle squad.

The effectiveness of the Marine/PF team results from the blending of the Marine's military professionalism with the PF's detailed knowledge of the local populace and terrain. A blending of talent occurs, beneficial to both PF and Marines. The Marines become familiar with their assigned area, more proficient in the Vietnamese language, and in effect "citizens" of their hamlets. From the Marines, PFs rapidly learn the tactics and self-confidence necessary to defeat the local guerrillas. The PFs graduate to a force capable of independently maintaining security for their area, and at the same time the Marine squad is redeployed to work with a new PF platoon. Since the program's inception, more than 75 redeployments have been made.

The success of the Combined Action Program is demonstrated by the fact that the VC have never been able to regain control of a hamlet or village once occupied by a CAP.

In summary, I view the Combined Action Program as a most valuable adjunct to the total effort in I Corps. The constant vigilance of the dedicated men in the Combined Action Platoons protects over 400,000 Vietnamese civilians from VC terrorist activities. The efforts of all the men of the Combined Action Program have contributed greatly to the peace and freedom of the citizens of I Corps.

* * *

FROM CG III MAF - They'll All Be Dead - December 12, 1969

An American or Republic of Vietnam fighting man should try not to give his life for his country. Instead, he should see to it that the enemy dies for his. Yet, men all over Vietnam have been losing their lives needlessly.

A Marine on an operation in a jungle area picks up an M-26 fragmentation grenade, "dropped by some guy in the squad," he thinks. A member of a patrol steps through a hole in a hedgerow. An Army engineer on a morning sweep of Highway 1 begins to check the same 10 potholes in the blacktop road he's been sweeping for a week, when somebody in the waiting column of trucks honks his horn impatiently. What do all of these men have in common? They'll all be dead in a matter of minutes.

Just after the Marine picks up the grenade, a firefight starts. He pulls the pin and throws the grenade. He'll never throw another. The enemy planted the grenade after removing the 4-7 second delay fuze and replacing it with a zero delay fuze.

The man at the hedgerow was very alert while moving along with his squad, then became momentarily careless. As he steps through the hedgerow, he feels the slight tug of a trip wire on his boot. It's too late now to check for trip wires. The explosion has already taken place.

The engineer sweeping the highway briefly forgets his professional training and hurries ahead. He steps in a shallow pothole of raw earth that he has checked so many times before. He will never take another step. The anti-vehicular mine with a light fuze setting explodes.

No matter what day you are reading this article, our past experience has shown that some men will die and others will be wounded by a mine or booby trap on this day. Many of these deaths and injuries could have been avoided.

What can we do to reduce these casualties? We can be alert-and stay alive. We can deny the enemy the U. S. casualties he needs so desperately. We can use the following guides. I'm sure that each of you can add to this check list.

First, know your stuff. All of us received a bill-fold-sized card when we arrived in Vietnam . . . a card called "Tips on VC/NVA Mines and Booby Traps." Read it and re-read it. Read "Lessons Learned." Leaders at every level must insure that every member of this command knows his stuff concerning mines and booby traps.

Next, control your ordnance. Never provide the enemy with material to build a mine or a booby trap. Claymores, mines and grenades of all types must be strictly controlled. Even M-16 rounds are used by the enemy as "foot popper" booby traps. Destroy duds. Call Explosive Ordnance Disposal men to disarm, destroy or evacuate those munitions you can't destroy. Do not use enemy ordnance. Do not use U. S. munitions that have been out of friendly control.

Finally, report all incidents. Complete and accurate reporting of incidents involving mines and booby traps broadens our base of knowledge. This knowledge will assist us in neutralizing the enemy's capability to inflict casualties on us. This knowledge will help us train our troops. This knowledge will save lives.

61

I am confident that our professionalism will beat the enemy at his own game. Let's make sure that he, not us, dies for his country.

* * *

FROM CG III MAF - Christmas, A Symbol of Peace - December 19, 1969

Christmas symbolizes peace, for on this day we celebrate the birth of the Prince of Peace. As we look around this war torn land, peace seems far away and the spirit of Christmas but a dim memory. The good cheer and closeness to family we associate with Christmas seems remote. Yet . . . the spirit of Christmas is here just as it was in Bethlehem those many years ago.

It was such a time and such a place amid a humble people that the Christ child was born. The people of Judea too, were threatened by cruel, ungodly individuals bent on world conquest. They too were called upon for great sacrifices. Today, as then, free men must fight to stay free; and we who fight for freedom will celebrate Christmas on the field of battle where "peace" has a special meaning.

For us, this Christmas will be a far different one than most Americans will celebrate. We will be separated from our home and family. Yet, this separation should make us mindful that Christmas is more than colored lights and tinsel. It is a day for rededication to the principles of peace.

Peace does not come easy. To have real meaning for our world, and the world of our children, peace must come with honor and be preserved by free men everywhere.

62

Our presence here in Vietnam as members of the military services is our contribution to the cause of peace and freedom. This contribution is the finest Christmas gift we can make not only to the Vietnamese people but to our families as well. By our actions we make it possible for Christmas to have meaning to the world. By our devotion to the cause of justice and freedom, we help bring about an earlier and fuller realization of that glorious message of the first Christmas: "Peace of Earth, Good Will to Men."

Christmas is a reminder to us of values that are eternal. I sense a terrible confusion in today's world as to the real life values. Therefore, Christmas, to me, gives all of us the opportunity to cast off our selfcenteredness and to focus our attention on spiritual values rather than on material goals. So let us remember in our hearts the wonderful story of Christmas ... the little child ... the shining star ... the manger ... the wise men from afar and the promise for us all. Let us hope that soon all mankind will join the Angelic Chorus in saying: "Glory to God in the Highest, and on earth peace, goodwill toward Men."

It is with these thoughts in mind that I extend to all my sincerest wishes for a happy and meaningful Christmas season.

* * *

CG III MAF - Grasping Revolutionary Development - December 26, 1969

During my two tours of duty in the Republic of Vietnam, I have seen some major changes taking place. Probably the one change which has impressed me most is the revolutionary development within the country.

63

Revolutionary development aims to bring to the people of the Republic of Vietnam-men, women and children-an awareness of their heritage as Vietnamese, their role as citizens, their partnership in national life.

A nation not yet 20 years old, the Republic of Vietnam finds itself faced with challenges that few, if any, other emerging new nations have had to cope.

The most obvious challenge, and the one we Soldiers, Sailors, Airmen and Marines are so deeply involved in today, is the armed conflict with the NVA. A second, equally important, challenge is the people's task of rebuilding their nation in the midst of this conflict.

We as U. S. citizens have never had to face the problems of the Vietnamese, because we were born in a nation that had successfully accomplished similar tasks. Here in Vietnam, we are tangible evidence of our nation's commitment to the proposition that this young nation should be afforded the opportunity to also enjoy freedom and independence.

Vietnam, like the United States, is made up of different types of people, living in varying environments. Throughout the years preceding 1954, when the Republic of Vietnam was founded, there was little national unity. The people regarded themselves as fishermen of the waters, citizens of the city, Montagnards in the mountains, farmers of the land, or whatever-depending upon where they lived and how they made their living.

One of the first things the Government of Vietnam recognized soon after its founding was that, if the new nation was to succeed, national unity must be established. The people had to see that they were citizens of the new Republic of Vietnam.

In order to bring the message to the people, the Revolutionary Development Cadre (RDC) idea was started. Today, in I Corps alone, there are 11,500 individual Revolutionary Development Cadre teams performing the mission of helping the people govern themselves as part of the Nation.

Members of the RDC wear black pajama-type garb which is the traditional dress of the farmer. This dress helps them relate to the people. RDC's are organized with 30 persons in a group and they are deployed in the contested hamlets of I Corps with a four-fold mission:

1. Identify and assist in the neutralization of the VC infrastructure in the hamlet.

2. Recruit, organize and train a People's Self Defense Force.

3. Help local officials establish an efficient local administration through popular elections.

4. Assist the people in assigning realistic priorities to their aspirations and to initiate self-help projects for the betterment of the village while being augmented by the various service agencies of the GVN.

The first two tasks relate directly to security and must be accomplished quickly.

In the final analysis, the Revolutionary Development Program of the RVN represents an effort to achieve a sense of belonging on the part of all the people as participating members of a free democracy. The people in the rural areas constitute 70 percent of the population. It is important for them to form their thoughts and voice their opinions to the government in Saigon.

65

Village self development in 1969, unlike past self help programs, is intended to bring about popular participation in local government and the development of a real community spirit. Thus, the success of the village self development program will not be measured only by the number of projects completed. The aim is to encourage the people to participate actively and freely with local officials in selecting and carrying out projects. Checkbooks are being used for the first time by village officials to control the flow of GVN and locally contributed funds. More than 2,000 projects have been authorized by the people themselves at public meetings and officials are acquiring fiscal and administrative skills.

Our mission at the village level is to free the people from Viet Cong interference, restore public security and assist all the people to actively participate in the national life of the country.

* * *

FROM CG III MAF - 1969-A Year of Accomplishment - January 2, 1970

Another year has passed. The war for freedom in Vietnam continues. But the war was different last year than the year before and will be different next year. Time passes quickly but time also buys us progress. There are those who protest that the Vietnam war is endless. In my view, these folks ignore past accomplishments, confuse the present state of affairs and fear the future because they lack the facts! We need only time, patience and perseverance to achieve an honorable victory.

The past gives us clues to use to consider the future. And last year was bountiful in clues to the bright future in this Republic. A detailed listing of significant events of 1969 would be far too voluminous for this column. But I think it important to review a few events of 1969 to show the trend of this war.

The major large scale operations come to all our minds first because they are dramatic in terms of achievement. The A Shau Valley was cleared of the main force North Vietnamese . . . Operation Dewey Canyon captured the greatest cache of enemy material of the war . . . Go Noi Island was cleared . . . Soldiers and Marines moved at will on the Khe Sanh plateau . . . Hiep Duc secured . . . the Que Son mountains dominated. These battlefield victories were gained by all of the U. S. forces in I Corps fighting alongside of our Korean allies and the stalwart Republic of Vietnam forces.

A country becomes united not in winning battles only but when its people can move about freely. And 1969 is noteworthy for the opening of air, rail and land lines of communication.

For the first time since U. S. tactical units came to the assistance of the Government of the Republic of Vietnam, the Danang to Hue train began a regular schedule. From time to time the enemy has blown the train or track, but each time the Vietnam Railroad Service made rapid repairs. The Danang-Hue train rolls on.

QL 1 is a first class highway. Commerce and people can move from Dong Ha-Quang Tri to Saigon over this road.

Adding a vital transportation link is Air Vietnam. Daily flights from Danang to Saigon bring the northern provinces quickly into contact with the nation's seat of government.

Just as indomitable as the surge of travel is the surge of democracy. Village and hamlet elections continue in spite of the enemy threats. Last September, the enemy razed over half the homes in An Phong Village. The next day, the villagers, undaunted, held a free election.

In 1969, President Thieu and our President Nixon read these signs of progress carefully and accurately. Then they announced the redeployment of approximately 60,000 U. S. troops. In I Corps Tactical Zone, the entire 3d Marine Division, certain 1st MAW units, selected Army support elements, and a sizeable number of Navy construction battalions departed.

The events of 1969 justified these moves-a major redeployment of U. S. fighting forces was possible because our Vietnamese comrades in Arms had shouldered more of the load.

1969 has been a good year . . . a year of which we all can be proud. With time, patience, and perseverance on our side, 1970 will surpass all our past accomplishments.

* * *

FROM CG III MAF - Preventive Maintenance-An All Hands Effort - January 9, 1970

Preventive maintenance is the name we give to the measures we use to keep our equipment in tip top shape. When the driver adds air to a low tire, when the rifleman cleans and lubricates his weapon, and when the cook cleans and refuels the galley immersion burners, they are performing preventive maintenance.

Too often we assume that only the specialists and technicians need to be concerned with maintenance matters. While it is true that the maintenance specialists and repairmen do undertake the technical work, the job of operating equipment properly, and keeping it in shape to continue operating, is an all hands effort.

A Marine and his gear are a team, and both halves of the team need to be ready. If you want your equipment to operate properly when the going gets tough, you better use some preventive maintenance before the fan stops ...

In the field you need to have your equipment functioning properly. You must be able to depend on your equipment. Keeping your gear in good working order is a basic for success. The skilled craftsman keeps his tools in excellent condition so he can do quality work. So I expect all Marines to maintain their gear in a constant state of readiness. Here in Vietnam under combat conditions, equipment failures can mean the difference between life and death.

Preventive maintenance takes care of the little problems before they become big ones. A driver of a multifuel truck who tries to move out in second gear instead of first is not using his equipment properly and his improper action will cause malfunction and breakdown. Preventive maintenance also means inspection and cleaning. Keeping condensation from affecting scopes and quadrants of fire control equipment requires that the gear be checked and cleaned daily, as well as being covered when not in use. The Marine who checks his ammo for short rounds, dents, cracks or corrosion is performing life saving preventive maintenance.

Preventive maintenance also involves performing the adjustments, minor repairs and testing for the purpose of keeping our equipment in operational condition, and correcting failures right away. Vehicle drivers should periodically check by hand, and, if necessary, tighten the mounting bolts and nuts on the universal joints or shock absorbers on his jeep, clean the battery posts, tighten the connecting cables, and check the electrolyte with a hydrometer to ensure the proper specific gravity necessary to prolong the life of wet cell batteries.

The preventive maintenance program is a command responsibility. That means all officers and NCO's must check. I mean inspections by fire team leaders and all the way up to Commanding Generals. Preventive Maintenance is truly an ALL HANDS EFFORT.

• • •

FROM CG III MAF - The Enemy in Vietnam - January 16, 1970

It has become apparent that the enemy is no match for the U. S. and allied forces in a conventional "set piece" battle, and the enemy realizes this too.

Since his disasterous "Tet" offensive in 1968, he has gradually reverted to the small scale type of operations that characterized the war in Vietnam during the early 1960's. The heart of his new doctrine appears to be the sapper attack. Since it is necessary to understand the enemy in order to discover his weaknesses, let's take a look at the sapper and how he operates.

Some people have the impression that the sapper has a sort of suicide mission similar to the "Kami Kaze" pilots of World War II. This comparison while possibly true in the past, certainly does not describe the sapper of today in Vietnam; he wants to accomplish his mission and stay alive. The sapper is a highly motivated, carefully selected, and thoroughly trained expert in the area of demolitions and penetration

70

techniques. The sapper is trained to slip undetected through the outer defenses of fortified areas and to launch his attacks from inside the perimeter. His principal weapon is a patient, detailed reconnaissance. The sachel charge and the vital element of surprise follow once he knows all about your defenses.

The sapper realizes that both his success and survival depend on the rapid destruction of preselected targets before he is discovered. For this reason, the sapper attack rarely lasts any longer than a few minutes. In order to confuse those in the target area, the sapper attack may be covered by a simultaneous attack by fire or even a ground assault. A diversion of this sort will cause the defenders to man bunkers along the perimeter while leaving the inner area lightly defended. Although casualties are generally caused by these attacks, target are normally command bunkers, artillery pieces, aircraft, and other facilities and materials.

Once the attack has begun, the sapper will not stop to engage individual soldiers, but moves along pre-planned routes to his targets and then out through the wire as quickly as possible. The difference between a successful operation and a dead sapper is the extent of his reconnaissance, the bad habits of the defenders, the absence of tanglefoot wire, and his knowledge of the inner perimeter. For these reasons, every attack is planned in the greatest detail. Reconnaissance is essential for success. Without a thorough knowledge of the target area, the sapper will not attack.

A recent Hoi Chanh, who had participated in over 40 sapper attacks during the preceding seven years, stated that unless he could breach the outer defenses and observe the enemy from the inner perimeter on at least 30 consecutive nights, he would not attack. During the reconnaissance phase, every detail must be noted ... the location of mines, booby traps and fighting positions, the number of guards, their habits and exact locations, routes to the targets and routes of withdrawl. Sappers are

71

too highly valued by the enemy to be committed without a high probability of success. The slightest change in the defensive posture of the target area may cause a postponement or cancellation of the intended attack.

Barbed wire, which is an important part of most defenses, is of little value unless used with properly laid out emplaced tanglefoot. Bear in mind that the sapper must be able to come and go through the wire, night after night without revealing his presence. A strip of "tanglefoot," six feet wide inside the double apron fence, no higher than four inches off the ground, pulled taut and securely staked down every 18 inches, will force the sapper to either go over the top of the wire or to cut the wire. Either course of action would be unsatisfactory to the sapper and force him to abandon his mission.

The best defense against the sapper is an alert soldier, sailor, airman or marine. Every effort must be made to deny the enemy information concerning our defenses. As in most situations, the little things make the difference. Don't smoke while standing guard. Avoid unnecessary movement and leave the radios back in the cantonment area. Avoid establishing any sort of discernible pattern or routine. Don't man the same positions night after night. Check the outer perimeter daily for possible signs of the enemy's presence. Inspect the mines and wire to be sure that they have not been tampered with. Relocate mines, booby traps and other devices frequently to confuse the potential attacker. These are just a few of the common sense things we can do to frustrate the sapper activity. Alertness is essential.

Always consider that your area, you as a possible sapper target. Remember the installation is being observed constantly. The sapper will not attack without a detailed knowledge of the target and unless he is reasonably sure of success.

The fact that you haven't been attacked for a long period doesn't mean you are in free-or that you are on R&R in country. This condition of quiet moves the probability of attack closer to you with each passing night. You can be certain you are being watched and that you will be attacked when you relax sufficiently ...

The sapper is a tough, professional foe, worthy of our respect, but he can be defeated by an alert, well trained fighting man who knows his tactics and is ready for him.

* * *

FROM CG III MAF – Discipline And Courtesy – January 23, 1970

Daily, the news media brings us accounts of individuals who demonstrate their contempt for an orderly, law abiding society.

By irresponsible acts, these persons are saying there is no place in today's world for restraint and discipline. They just "do their thing" regardless. But without restraint and discipline, there can be no freedom. And, without freedom, there can be no real progress in the world.

No group-civilian or military-can long survive without discipline . . . self-discipline and the rule of law, or if you will, the discipline of laws ... the respect for the rights of others.

Discipline is the soul of our Corps. Without it, "mobocracy" would result. Discipline transforms a mob into a group of law abiding citizens ... and for those citizens in the armed forces of our government discipline makes them an effective force.

73

Many of our young men enlisted in an effort to find stability; and in doing so, they discovered discipline and real-life values.

In joining our ranks, they dedicated themselves to the principles for which our country stands and which our Corps has defended over the years. These young Americans quickly adapt themselves to the orderliness of our organization. And by their esprit de corps, they express their belief in their leaders. As leaders, it is our sacred trust never to let them down, in garrison or in combat.

How do we effectively maintain discipline? This is what our 13th Commandant, Major General John A. Lejeune, was concerned with when, in 1920, he wrote Letter No. 1 to all Marine Corps Officers. General Lejeune summed up, in one eloquent paragraph, how a leader can maintain discipline and retain the respect of his men. Here is what he wrote:

"Be kindly and just in your dealing with your men. Never play favorites. Make them feel that justice tempered with mercy may always be counted on. This does not mean a slackening of discipline. Obedience to orders and regulations must always be insisted upon, and good conduct on the part of the men exacted. Especially should this be done with reference to the civilian inhabitants of foreign countries in which Marines are serving."

The discipline among our ranks is direct measurement of the quality of our leadership. The alert, intellectually curious, just leader gives our Corps a disciplined fire team, squad, battalion or amphibious force.

Joined to discipline is courtesy. Courtesy and discipline must be inseparable. As Emerson wrote: "Life is not so short but there is always time for courtesy . . ." For example, that automatic gesture of courtesy known as the salute is also a mark of discipline. Yet if this simple act is rendered only through of reprisal, real discipline is lacking. A salute cheerfully and smartly executed is a sure sign of esprit de corps.

Unhesitating obedience to lawful orders in combat is an essential ingredient for success. Marine Corps discipline instills this quality in us all. We learn also to respect the rights and needs of others. When we have become a true brother-in-arms, tested in combat, we become firmly convinced that discipline and courtesy are inseparable.

Raymond W. Miller put it this way. "While it is priceless, courtesy is simple and elementary as the verse we used to read in children's books which goes . . . To every heart there are two little keys. . . "Thank you, Sir," and "If you please."

We preserve our American Heritage of Liberty---under God and within the law--when we are ever mindful of the rights and needs of others--and when we practice self-discipline and exploit the contagiousness of courtesy.

. . .

FROM CG III MAF - Amphibious Warfare-A Bright Future - January 30, 1970

In 1915 the British made an amphibious landing in the Middle East on the Gallipoli Peninsula of Turkey. Nine months later the unsuccessful British force withdrew from those shores, having failed to accomplish its objectives.

British Commodore Sir Roger Keyes, second in command at Gallipoli, stated in

75

1943 that "among the most valuable lessons we learned from the original landings was the folly of attempting to storm a defended beach in daylight."

When he made this statement, Marines had already assaulted the Japanese-defended beach at Tulagi, proving the effectiveness of amphibious warfare. World War II saw a succession of amphibious operations in the Pacific, Africa and Europe by U. S. forces and our allies in the march to victory.

In April of 1945, Okinawa was the scene of the largest amphibious operation conducted in the Pacific Theater. Six Marine and Army divisions and over 1,100 naval vessels took part. Among the units going ashore were the First Marine Division and the Army XXIV Corps.

A few months later the world was witness to the awesome effect of the atomic bomb. Certain military and civilian leaders believed the atomic bomb spelled an end to amphibious warfare. While it was doubtful that operations on the scale of the Okinawa landing would be repeated, the Marine Corps continued to improve and update amphibious doctrine.

In September of 1950, the importance of amphibious operations was reaffirmed by the landing at Inchon, spearheaded by the First Marine Division. The assault was decisive, outflanking North Korean forces pressing hard against U. N. forces in the Pusan Perimeter.

During the past four and a half years Marines of the III Marine Amphibious Force have been engaged in counter-insurgency operations. To Marines this has meant a complete dedication to fighting the enemy in the jungles, hills and rice paddies of Vietnam. Actions at Khe Sanh, Dong Ha or An Hoa provided little time or

76

necessity for the men involved to think about purely amphibious operations. However, in this conflict, Marines have seen action assaulting across the beach or moving inland by helicopterborne ship-to-shore movements.

Professionally, the individual Marine was prepared. One of our missions in the Corps is "to conduct such operations as the President may direct." Our Corps has been traditionally a force in readiness: service with the American Expeditionary Force in France in World War I, guarding the mails during the 1920's and conducting counter-insurgency operations in Latin America between the world wars are examples. Although our effort in Vietnam has been on a much larger scale, it has not been unlike those Latin America counter-insurgency operations.

We have applied our amphibious doctrine to our operations in Vietnam. More than sixty amphibious landings have been conducted by the Navy-Marine Corps team, inflicting in excess of 6,500 killed upon the enemy. Basic to these operations has been the Amphibious Ready Group (ARG) composed of amphibious U. S. Navy Ships, and the Special Landing Force (SLF), composed of a battalion landing team and a squadron of support helicopters.

Operation Starlite in Southern I Corps in September 1965 inaugurated this series of amphibious operations. A combination of vertical and beach assaults successfully moved across positions of the 1st NVA Regiment. The enemy sustained 699 casualties, eliminating the regiment as an effective force. Operation Starlite proved once again the soundness of Marine Corps training and our amphibious warfare doctrine, thereby setting the stage for subsequent operations. The most recent amphibious success was a combined US/ROK Marine Corps operation, in September, which inflicted 294 casualties upon VC forces.

Marines have frequently applied the principles and techniques of amphibious

77

doctrine to operations conducted in the mountainous jungles of Vietnam. For example, many aspects of Operation Dewey Canyon were similar to an amphibious operation. The Amphibious Ready Group was represented by Vandergrift Combat Base and the individual ships by LZ's at VCB. The Direct Air Support Center at Task Force Hotel, located at VCB, performed functions identical to those of the Helicopter Direction Center aboard the LPH. A control organization similar to the amphibious tactical logistical group directed helicopters to pick up pre-netted supplies from a designated point on the LPH deck (the Logistics Support Area at VCB) and instructed them to deliver their loads to specified LZ's at the head of the Ashau Valley forty kilometers southwest. During flight over the inhospitable jungle mountains under marginal weather conditions (ship to shore movement) the helicopters were directed by the VCB DASC (HDC) until they were turned over to an Air Support Radar Team at FSB Cunningham which controlled the final approach into the operational areas. Landing of supplies at the company level was under control of Shore Party personnel attached to the companies. Many other analogies can be drawn between Dewey Canyon and an amphibious operation, but this gives you a good idea of what I'm talking about.

Our experience in Vietnam has demonstrated the value of amphibious operations. The enemy has been denied use of the immediate coastal area by the threat posed by the SLF. When the enemy has chosen to ignore the threat he has been subject to surprise attack from the seaward. The ARG/SLF has shown itself to be a flexible force, achieving tactical success through mobility and effective employment of naval gunfire, air and artillery.

Since 1775, the Marine Corps has been engaged in amphibious warfare. Vietnam has reaffirmed the soundness of our doctrine. When trouble flares, the Corps will be ready. Continuing developments in the doctrine, techniques and equipment of amphibious warfare assures us of a place in the defense forces of our country as a force in readiness.

* * *

FROM CG III MAF – What Chieu Hoi Means To You – February 6, 1970

Chieu Hoi means "Open Arms." It is the name of the program by which the enemy can surrender or rally honorably and be given a new start in life under the Government of the Republic of Vietnam. A rallier under this program is called a Hoi Chanh.

The Chieu Hoi Program reduces the enemy strength while augmenting the Republic of Vietnam Armed Forces (RVNAF) and the Free World Military Assistance Forces (FWMAF). The Chieu Hoi Program saves lives as it helps win the war.

If large numbers of Viet Cong, Viet Cong infrastructure and North Vietnam soldiers rally to the Government of Vietnam, the enemy's morale and combat effectiveness are weakened. The RVNAF and FWMAF psychological operations units spend a great amount of time and effort encouraging the enemy to rally. But the support of every soldier, sailor, airman and marine in I Corps Tactical Zone is needed. In our dealings with the local populace, we should understand the meaning of the Chieu Hoi Program and the procedures of rallying.

The rallier, called a Hoi Chanh, passes through several agencies prior to his arrival st a province Chieu Hoi Center. Each of these agencies gains valuable intelligence from the Hoi Chanh. Through him we have found large caches of weapons . . . weapons that will never be used against us. Also the Hoi Chanh has helped to identify and fix enemy units. He has alerted us to future enemy attacks.

In addition to his contribution of combat intelligence, the Chieu Hoi by his action of rallying has shown an honest desire to become a useful citizen of the Republic of Vietnam.

If he desires, the Chieu Hoi is taught vocational skills; and he and his family begin a new productive life in a resettlement village or he may enter the RVNAF, the Regional Forces, the Popular Forces or join a Revolutionary Development Cadre. He may become a member of an Armed Propaganda Team. Some have become Kit Carson Scouts. No one knows the enemy better than a Hoi Chanh, because he was one. These are but a few of the paths open to the rallier who comes back to the Government side.

Approximately $400 (U.S.) is spent for each Hoi Chanh during his 45-60 day residence in a Chieu Hoi Center. Considering how much is spent each day in fighting this war, the Chieu Hoi Program is a bargain indeed. However, the biggest saving is not in money but in lives. No friendly lives are lost when a Hoi Chanh rallies but the enemy loses a man.

There were 47,023 Hoi Chanhs in 1969 . . . 5,996 of these in I Corps Tactical Zone. This means the enemy has lost a force of 47,023 men . . . a severe loss for any army in a single year.

There are a few simple rules we should follow in dealing with Hoi Chanhs. These rules require very little of us, but they are most important to the Hoi Chanh. When he decides to rally he makes one of the biggest decisions of his life. The enemy counter-propaganda against the Chieu Hoi Program is on his mind. He is frightened and apprehensive of our actions during his reception. We must overcome this fear by following these simple guidelines:

1. Let all people claiming to be a Hoi Chanh come in safely.

2. Welcome the Hoi Chanh and keep him separated from detainees who will be turned over to RVNAF as prisoners of war.

3. Give the Hoi Chanh a receipt for all weapons he turns in.

4. Take the Hoi Chanh to the unit intelligence officer for processing and further transfer to the district or province Chieu Hoi Center.

Without the Chieu Hoi Program, the enemy would have no chance for a new life. He would have to continue to fight until killed or captured. And some of us would die in the process. Chieu Hoi means new life for the Hoi Chanh. And to us . . . Chieu Hoi means a new ally where once stood an old foe.

* * *

ANNIVERSARY MESSAGE

On 1 February the 1st Marine Division completes 29 years of illustrious service to our corps and our country. It was the first of the Marine divisions to engage the enemy in World War II. During that war, the Marines of the division were proudly called the "old breed." When the Korean War began, the 1st Marine Division was ready and again distinguished itself in battle earning the title the "new breed." In 1966 the 1st Marine Division was deployed to the Republic of Vietnam and, upholding the traditions of the past, has proven itself as the "Fighting Breed."

In the jungles and on the hills and beaches of Vietnam, the 1st Marine Division has added many glorious and heroic pages to the history of the division and the history of the corps. To the many battles of old are now added Union, Taylor Common,

Allenbrook, Mameluke Thrust, Mead River, Oklahoma Hills, Pipestone Canyon, and many others. Each of these operations has demonstrated again the dedication, the fighting spirit, and the courage of the Marine of the 1st Marine Division.

I congratulate you on your anniversary and wish you continued success in your "fight for right and freedom."

* * *

FROM CG III MAF - You, Mr. Ambassador - February 13, 1970

Although the title, "Ambassador", does not appear in your enlistment contract or commission oath, it correctly defines the task of every man who wears the uniform of his country. As a member of the United States Armed Forces you are a representative of America, and everything for which our nation stands. You are a symbol of the American way of life. Indeed, you are an "Ambassador."

You have an awesome responsibility, Mr. Ambassador. You represent America in the eyes of the world. Here in Vietnam everything the American military man does--from providing people with soap to searching for the enemy--can create admiration for our way of life or cause resentment and ill will. In the eyes of the people, whether they are children or adults, soldiers, or farmers, residents or refugees, we tell the story of the United States. Our actions, our words, our attitudes communicate to the people of Vietnam what our country is really like.

You have no easy task, Mr. Ambassador. To be effective, it is not enough for the American fighting man to be a skilled combatant; he must also be a worthy representative of the concern of our nation for the freedom, well-being, and dignity of all men. The impression that you as an individual convey to the Vietnamese people may be the only picture they have of America. Your actions mold their opinions.

You, Mr. Ambassador, are the reflection of the United States in the eyes of the citizens of the Republic of Vietnam. How accurately you represent the people of our nation, how well you live our American beliefs before their eyes, will determine the future of freedom and democracy in Southeast Asia. You can tell the people of the nations throughout the world what freedom and equality are, but only your actions prove you mean what you say.

On July 4th, 1776, when American patriots published the unanimous declaration of the thirteen united states of America, they told the world that they believed that all men are created equal, that they are endowed by their creator with certain inalienable rights, that among these are life, liberty, and the pursuit of happiness. When our forefathers took their stand for freedom at Concord Bridge and Lexington Green, that message echoed across the ocean. When the Liberty Bell "proclaimed freedom throughout the land", the echo encircled the globe. Today, Mr. Ambassador, you are that echo. It is your day to day positive actions that keep the torch of freedom burning brightly for all the world to see.

The importance of your role as ambassador is great and far reaching. We live in an age of revolution; an age in which conflicting ideologies compete for the hearts and minds of people everywhere. The image that world has of our United States and what America stands for is what people see when they see you! What the citizen of Vietnam thinks of our American principles of justice, freedom, and equality is determined by your actions.

America's fighting man is the most important ambassador our nation has. You

83

are doing a magnificent job. You are meeting the challenge. I commend you. Never forget that the hopes and dreams of all who cherish freedom rest on your shoulders. Your role is well expressed in Article VI of the Code of Conduct: "I will never forget that I am an American fighting man, responsible for my actions, and dedicated to the principles which made my country free. I will trust in my God and in the United States of America."

* * *

FROM CG III MAF - Drug Abuse-The Price is High - February 20, 1970

Today we live in a society in which the use of drugs is common.

Our radios say "take an aspirin break" and our TVs advise us that a deacidifier is just the thing to cure the blahs. Our magazines extol the virtues of this or that beverage, and all media of communications are used to lure us into "Cigarette Country" with a hint of mint, or a promise that our taste will be springtime fresh.

No, we Americans don't question the use of drugs. We know certain drugs are required for medical purposes. We also accept as fact that drugs can produce any kind of desired effect--from springtime--to happiness--to the inner calm and success .... all coming from that little, gentle, blue pill.

Our problem is trying to decide which drugs are right and which are wrong. It seems most people think they alone have an unerring ability to pick what is right and what is wrong. They think that the acceptable drugs are the ones they use; the unacceptable, the ones you use.

But let's rise above the emotion which clouds this issue and cut to the heart of the drug problem. Most important, we must realize the powerful influence society has to play in the drugs of choice. We all must live in society, must be a part of society and, therefore, must be subject to the rules of our society, whether or not they be codified as laws. None of us can hope for any lasting happiness, if we flaunt these laws.

Next, consider why we use drugs. Many will say, "I like them" or "they make me feel good." I question both these answers.

You who smoke cigarettes--do they really taste good? Perhaps the one after each meal does. Then why do you smoke 20 or 40 a day, when only 3 taste good?

The use of drugs, both legal and illegal, is far more than a matter of "feel good" or "taste good." It is tied in with more basic wants, both psychological and sociological . . . . wants such as the need to be accepted by our friends and to be considered easy going and fun loving--to be "cool." Yet, is it really "cool" to numb our senses and possibly harm our bodies permanently? Is it worth the price to be "cool"? When we answer this question honestly, drugs will no longer be a problem.

Marijuana is declared illegal by our society. Penalties for its use are severe-5 to 20 years imprisonment. The serviceman may get either a Dishonorable Discharge or Bad Conduct Discharge, in addition to other punishments.

Yet people continue to experiment in its use. Why? Surely marijuana can't be good enough to risk life-long punishment. It isn't. But, for reasons known only to themselves, some people believe they prove their manhood by using it. It makes them one of the "group." For this, the immature person will risk anything.

There is a danger that marijuana will rob a person of his self-control, his sex

85

drive and, eventually, his will to succeed. But he will gamble in order to be held in high regard by his marijuana-smoking friends.

Regardless of the drug you may take, ask yourself-do I really want this, or am I just trying to impress someone? Am I getting into a habit which has no real meaning? Ask yourself what dangers this drug holds, not only the physical dangers, but the legal dangers? How could anything be good enough to risk ruining the rest of your natural life?

Some people complain about the military draft takes two years out of your lives. Yet these same people willingly endanger their remaining years just to prove to someone that they're doing their "thing". What a waste!

Know what drugs can do. Know what the law can do to you. Make a logical decision to avoid throwing your life away for a cheap thrill.

* * *

FROM CG III MAF - **Physical Fitness-Key To Self-Confidence** - **February 27, 1970**

In combat the measure of physical fitness often is the measure of survival. There are no "time outs" in a fire fight.

Our troops in the field slog through paddy mud and struggle up jungled mountains . . . in monsoon rain and 100-degree heat. They bend under the weight of flak jackets, weapons, rations and ammo. But when they meet the enemy, they are physically ready. To be weak at this moment is to become a casualty.

When a Marine enters boot camp, physical conditioning begins. When he comes to a line outfit in Vietnam, he understands why. But not all may serve in these units. Some must serve on staffs, and in support and service organizations.

We, then, are the ones who must remind ourselves that physical fitness is a personal responsibility. There no longer is a drill instructor to encourage us. Each is his own physical fitness instructor.

Someone once said: "Health is a gift, but you have to work to keep it." Neglect your physical well-being and the "gift" goes-and, with it, your self-confidence.

But the self-disciplined man guards his gift of health. He relieves mental tension with physical exertion. You will find him on handball and tennis courts. You see him jogging around a rear area compound. He's playing basketball or pressing a set of bar bells. And when he returns to work, his mind is clear. Professional problems become a challenge rather than a headache. The administrator who coined the phrase "a bucket of worms" probably got his exercise in the club. The man who is physically tough is mentally tough. He doesn't think in terms of "worms."

I once read about a businessman who felt his mind was coming apart under the tension of competition. He went to a close friend, a doctor, to seek rather pathetic medical advice. He asked his friend to prescribe a method of death which would not appear as suicide. The patient did not want to embarrass his family when he escaped the pressures of life. Shaken at first, the doctor composed himself and and prescribed running. He told his sick friend that, at his age, his heart couldn't withstand the physical strain. Within two months, the businessman disproved the doctor's prognosis. He had exercised himself back into the world.

This was an extreme case. But it shows the power of physical well-being in shoring up our self-confidence.

Those of us in the rear areas, perform well only when we feel well . . . when we are confident in ourselves, and in the job we do. The work we do could well mean the difference between life and death for the trooper on patrol. He is confident as he faces the enemy. We who support him must be equally confident in our abilities. Anything short of complete self-confidence is unacceptable. And the key to self-confidence is physical fitness.

* * *

Command To Shift In I Corps Area

SAIGON-Reorganization of U. S. forces in the I Corps Tactical Zone area will result in III MAF becoming a subordinate command within U. S. XXIV Corps effective March 9. This reverses the present command arrangement which places XXIV Corps under III MAF.

With the redeployment of the 3d Mar. Div. and the 26th Marine Regimental Landing Team, U. S. Army forces have become the predominant U. S. military element in the I Corps area. The command realignment reflects this shift in field force structure.

Lt. Gen. Herman Nickerson, Jr., U. S. Marine Corps, will depart approximately March 9 for the United States. His successor, Maj. Gen. Keith B. McCutcheon, U. S. Marine Corps, who has been nominated for lieutenant general will assume command of III MAF as the commanding general of a sub-element of XXIV Corps. XXIV Corps is commanded by Lt. Gen. Melvin Zais, U.S. Army.

The XXIV Corps was activated as a provisional corps in March 1968, and redesignated as XXIV Corps in August, 1968, to control the U.S. forces in the northern portion of the I Corps area. It has been a subordinate element of III MAF since its establishment. III MAF was established in 1965 to control all U.S. forces in I Corps. At the time of its establishment, U.S. Marine forces were the predominate U.S. military element in the area.

The activation of the Americal Division in 1967 began a buildup of U.S. Army forces within I Corps which eventually involved the commitment of the 1st Bde., of the 5th Div. (Mechanized), the 101st Airborne Div. (Airmobile), and the 1st Cavalry Div. (Airmobile). The 1st Cavalry Div. (Airmobile) was later deployed to the III Corps Tactical Zone.

* * *

FROM CG III MAF - Tam Biet

Nearly 34 years ago I first came to the Orient as a second lieutenant with the Fourth Marines in Shanghai, China. The command part of my career as a Marine Officer began there and it is now nearing an end at Danang on the China Sea. Soon I shall be retired from the Marine Corps. My time on active duty has come full cycle.

The turmoil that was the Asia of my youth is even more volatile today. But today there is a difference. There is hope. Today the peoples of the ancient cultures of Asia have entered the 20th century while keeping their heritage intact. The communists would bring 20th century materialism to Asians, but at the cost of cultural obliteration. I am convinced that this is the blind spot of the communists . . . their nemesis. The people of the Republic of Vietnam have resisted communism with the help of the Free World. And they are winning. With perseverance and patience on the part of their allies, this war will be concluded successfully . . . and the heritage of the Vietnamese people established.

Already, military victory is beyond the grasp of the North Vietnamese and the Viet Cong. The determination of the South Vietnamese, which is best exemplified by the People's Self Defense Forces, is frustrating the guerrillas' attempt to intimidate and terrorize the people. The Republic of Vietnam has become one nation with a common purpose--freedom.

As I prepare to leave the Republic of Vietnam, memories crowd around me. But I look forward to a future of service in the cause of freedom. Those of you under my command have filled me with great pride as I have observed your courage and service to God and Country. My Vietnamese comrades have given me an unshakeable hope for the future of Asia.

It is with humility and hope that I leave the III Marine Amphibious Force . . .and soon the active list of the Marine Corps. For these gifts of spirit, I salute you.

* * *

Official Biography

LIEUTENANT GENERAL HERMAN NICKERSON, JR., USMC (RETIRED)

Lieutenant General Herman Nickerson, Jr., who served his last tour of active duty in the Marine Corps as Commanding General, III Marine Amphibious Force/Senior Advisor, I Corps Tactical Zone, and I Corps Coordinator for United States and Free World Military Assistance Forces, in the Republic of Vietnam, was honored in retirement ceremonies held at the Marine Barracks, 8th and I Streets, S.E., in Washington, D.C., on 31 March 1970.

As a colonel during the Korean War, General Nickerson was awarded the Army Distinguished Service Cross, the Nation's second highest combat award, for extraordinary heroism on 31 May 1951, as Commanding Officer of the 7th Marines, 1st Marine Division. His citation states in part:

> Learning that two of his battalions were heavily engaged and that the enemy was grouping for a counterattack, Colonel Nickerson unhesitatingly left the comparative safety of his command post and fearlessly moved forward over rugged mountainous terrain, under intense enemy mortar and artillery fire, to the most forward elements of his command. Unmindful of his personal safety, he advanced to an exposed vantage point under heavy enemy fire and through his brilliant guidance, his troops repulsed the ferocious counter-attack, taking the offensive and overwhelming the fanatical foe to secure the high ground dominating the vital road junction of Yang-gu.

Herman Nickerson, Jr., was born 30 July 1913, in Boston Massachusetts, and graduated from high school in Arlington, Massachusetts. Following graduation from Boston University where he was a member of the ROTC unit for four years, he resigned an Army Reserve commission to accept appointment as a Marine second lieutenant on 10 July 1935.

After completing Basic School at the Philadelphia Navy Yard in February 1936, Lieutenant Nickerson embarked for Shanghai, China, where he served for two and a half years with the 4th Marines. While in China, he was promoted to first lieutenant in August 1938. On his return to the United States in November 1938, he served as Commanding Officer of the Marine Detachment at the Naval Air Station, Seattle, Washington. Joining the 2d Defense Battalion in September 1940, he served with them in San Diego, California, and Parris Island, South Carolina. In May 1941, he was promoted to captain while on temporary duty under instruction at the Coast Artillery School, Fort Monroe, Virginia.

In December 1941, following the attack on Pearl Harbor, Captain Nickerson departed Parris Island for San Diego with the 2d Defense Battalion to join the 2d Marine Brigade overseas. Arriving on American Samoa in January 1942, he served consecutively as Battery Commander, Group Executive Officer, and finally Group Commander, Three-Inch Antiaircraft Artillery Group. While overseas, he was promoted to major in May 1942 and to lieutenant colonel in June 1943. He returned to the United States in July 1943.

That October, Lieutenant Colonel Nickerson was assigned to Marine Corps Schools, Quantico, Virginia, as Commanding Officer of the Ordnance School, and subsequently completed the Command and Staff School. In February 1945, he joined the 4th Infantry Training Regiment at Camp Pendleton, California, and again embarked for duty in the Pacific area, serving as Ordnance Officer, 4th Marine Division, and Executive Officer, 25th Marines. He later saw duty as Ordnance Officer with the III Amphibious Corps in Tientsin, China, and following dissolving of the III Amphibious Corps, served as Division Ordnance Officer and Division Legal Officer, respectively, of the 1st Marine Division.

In January 1947, on his return to the United States Lieutenant Colonel Nickerson began a three-year assignment at the Marine Corps Recruit Depot, Parris Island, serving consecutively as Assistant G-3, Recruit Training Battalion Commander, Weapons Training Battalion Commander, and Assistant Chief of Staff, G-3. He also saw temporary duty from January through August 1949 as a U.S. Military Observer with the United Nations Mission in Palestine and seven Arab states. Following this, he completed the Armed Forces Staff College, Norfolk, Virginia, and was promoted to colonel in July 1950. That same month, upon the outbreak of hostilities in Korea, he departed for the Far East.

From August 1950 to April 1951, Colonel Nickerson served as advisor on Marine Corps matters, General Headquarters, Far East Command, and also performed temporary additional duty in Korea. For conspicuous gallantry in September 1950 as Liaison Officer, 1st Marines, 1st Marine Division, during the advance along the Inchon-Seoul highway and the Han River crossing, he was awarded the Silver Star Medal. In April 1951, he became Commanding Officer of the 7th Marines in Korea, serving in this capacity through September 1951. During the early part of this period, he earned both the Legion of Merit with Combat "V" and, subsequently, the Army Distinguished Service Cross.

Colonel Nickerson was named Inspector of Fleet Marine Force, Pacific, in October 1951. In March 1952, he returned to Marine Corps Schools, Quantico, where he served as Director, Advance Base Problem Section, until June 1954, and Director Senior School, until July 1956. He served next as Assistant Chief of Staff, G-3, Fleet Marine Force, Pacific, at Pearl Harbor from August 1956 to December 1957. In January 1958, he joined Fleet Marine Force, Atlantic, at Norfolk, as Assistant Chief of Staff, G-3.

Transferred to Headquarters Marine Corps in September 1958, Colonel Nickerson served as Special Assistant to the Fiscal Director until April 1959, when he was named Fiscal Director of the Marine Corps. He was promoted to brigadier general on 1 January 1959.

While at Headquarters Marine Corps, General Nickerson was elected President of the American Society of Military Comptrollers in 1959 and again in 1960. He completed his tour of duty as Fiscal Director of the Marine Corps in May 1962. That June he assumed command of the 1st Marine Division at Camp Pendleton. He was promoted to major general, 1 July 1962.

In April 1963, General Nickerson joined the Marine Corps Supply Center, Barstow, California, as Commanding General. He served as Commanding General, Marine Corps Base, Camp Lejeune, North Carolina, from June 1965 until September 1966.

Ordered to the Republic of Vietnam in October 1966, General Nickerson commanded the 1st Marine Division until May 1967, earning the Distinguished Service Medal, and for service as Deputy Commander, III Marine Amphibious Frce from June 1967 to October 1967, he was awarded a gold star in lieu of a second Legion of Merit with Combat "V".

Upon his return to the United States in November 1967, he served briefly as Assistant Chief of Staff, G-3, at Headquarters Marine Corps. In January 1968, he was assigned duty as Director of Personnel/Deputy Chief of Staff (Manpower), and was promoted to the rank of lieutenant general on 12 January 1968. He retired from active duty, 31 March 1970.

Detached from Headquarters Marine Corps in March 1969, General Nickerson returned to the Republic of Vietnam for duty as Commanding General, III Marine Amphibious Force, and earned a gold star in lieu of a second Distinguished Service Medal.

A list of his medals and decorations includes: the Army Distinguished Service Cross; the Distinguished Service Medal with one gold star in lieu of a second award; the Silver Star Medal; the Legion of Merit with Combat "V" and Gold Star in lieu of a second award; the Bronze Star Medal; the Air Medal; the Presidential Unit Citation with two bronze stars indicative of second and third awards; the China Service Medal with one bronze star; the American Defense Service Medal; the Asiatic-Pacific Campaign Medal; the American Campaign Medal; the World War II Victory Medal; the Navy Occupation Service Medal; the National Defense Service Medal with one bronze star; the Korean Service Medal with one silver star in lieu of five bronze stars; the Vietnam Service Medal with three bronze stars; the Korean Chung Mu Medal; the Vietnamese National Order; the Vietnamese Army Distinguished Service Order; the Cross of Gallantry with three Palms; the National Order of Vietnam, 4th and 5th Class; the United Nations Service Medal (Korea); the United Nations Service Medal (Palestine); two Korean Presidential Unit Citations; and the Republic of Vietnam Campaign Medal.